IT TAKES MORE
THAN BALLS

IT TAKES MORE THAN BALLS

The Savvy Girls' Guide to Understanding and Enjoying Baseball

Deidre Silva and Jackie Koney

Skyhorse Publishing

Skyhorse Publishing books may be purchased in bulk at special discounts for sales promotion, corporate gifts, fund raising, or educational purposes. Special editions can also be created to specifications. For details, contact Special Sales Department, Skyhorse Publishing, 555 Eighth Avenue, Suite 903, New York, NY 10018 or info@skyhorsepublishing.com.

www.skyhorsepublishing.com

Library of Congress Cataloging-in-Publication Data

Silva, Deidre.
    It takes more than balls : the savvy girls' guide to understanding and enjoying baseball / Deidre Silva and Jackie Koney.
        p. cm.
    ISBN 978-1-60239-631-9 (alk. paper)
1. Baseball—Social aspects—United States. 2. Baseball fans—United States. 3. Baseball for women—United States. I. Koney, Jackie. II. Title.
GV867.64.S55 2007
796.357—dc22   2007051102

10 9 8 7 6 5 4 3 2 1

Printed in Canada

To our Moms, who died before they had a chance to talk us out of this.
And to our Dads, who were left telling us it'd all be Okay.

"There isn't a court or field in this country that, given the chance, I haven't stormed. Only once, though, I was given a shot at a major-league field. The day started when I snuck out of work early to watch the Seattle Mariners play the California Angels in the one-game playoff to decide the 1995 American League West. When the Mariners won, hundreds of fans jumped onto the field. I didn't hesitate. I sized up my competition: a frazzled usher standing on the grass behind third base. He started to make a move toward the wall once he realized that I was preparing to hurdle it. He tracked me as I dropped down about five feet, and, when I landed on the field, he sprung into action. Ah, a sportsman! I faked right, went left, and got clear. Moments later I was standing on second base in the middle of the Kingdome kicking at some dirt and thinking, 'Yep, here I am.' Other fans meandered around the infield; some pretended to catch balls at the warning track. A couple others stood on the pitcher's mound and talked on cellphones. Satisfied with myself, I climbed back into the stands by first base and headed out the front door. Oh—and I did all of this while wearing three-inch heels, a blue tartan skirt and carrying a smart briefcase. The memory of the usher's gape-mouth expression still makes me giggle."

—Deidre, 40

"It was 1999. Tiger Stadium's final season and Mom's seventy-fifth birthday provided two perfectly good reasons for family and friends to gather from across the country for a weekend of parties including, as it turned out, one last ballgame together. Recounting a few memories from that tattered but treasured stadium kept our minds off the ferocious beating the Oakland A's were administering to the Detroit Tigers. Dad told us a story from his childhood when he saw Babe Ruth and was surprised to see that the Babe was pot-bellied instead of having the physique of a world-class athlete. We remembered the euphoria of the 1984 World Series season, when my future husband snagged a piece of Tiger Stadium sod and kept it alive in his college dorm shower well into spring training of 1985. There were the memories of snowflakes and spiked hot chocolate on opening day, sunburns in August, my friends and me getting acquainted with the margarita vendors, and falling in love under the Budweiser sign in the last row of the centerfield bleachers."

—Jackie, 42

Contents

power, Roberto Clemente, Nicaraguan earthquake, cleanup guy, Lou Gehrig, Brooks Robinson, Boog Powell, Bob Boone.

player, tricky situations, Cone's collapse, pitching woes, "Donnie Baseball," young A-Rod, batting around the order, Will he make it?!?, cynical minds, Mike Hargrove.

Poison apple story, carpool schedule, Jack Norworth, baseball fables, Polo Grounds, Katie Casey, had the fever, Harry Caray's throaty rendition, flatline, state your mind and run, dicey situations.

Introduction

We love baseball, and we want to share with you how we've grown to enjoy baseball even though we have never played the game. Sure, throughout the years we've played softball, on the occasional and casual outing, with various company-sponsored teams. Jackie holds her own at first base, steadying herself when one of our teammates throws the ball hard at her, expecting her to catch it, of course. And it is a good bet she will. Sure, there's the occasional yelp, but she's a pretty tough jock. Deidre, who happens to be a lifelong soccer player, instinctively stops ground balls with her feet. She has bruises and lumps to show for it. Our teammates carry beverage cups to the outfield and set them down, balancing them in the tall grass. Sometimes they teeter over (the cups, that is), and that's our team's definition of an error. None of this experience counts toward a basic knowledge of baseball, but it certainly is fun.

And we thoroughly enjoy watching games. Watching them on TV is fine, but going to the stadium is often better. Sometimes we get nostalgic and sit on Deidre's back porch listening to a game through the crackle of a transistor radio while sipping gimlets, and eating barbequed ribs. OK, you caught us. We don't know how to make gimlets—but the barbeque claim is

verifiable. Anyway, the way the two of us drink in baseball is similar to how some people appreciate music or art: enjoying them without apology, even if they've never played a note or sketched an apple.

We don't get unduly upset about baseball, even though like most fans, we care about teams we've grown up with or have grown to love. Nor is our standard of currency based on swapping baseball knowledge. Of course, that's not saying we don't know a lot about baseball; it's just that researching and debating baseball's multitudinous particulars is not how we choose to spend our hard earned spare time. That said, we're happy when our team wins and bummed when they lose. Then there are times when we wonder, the next day, "Which team won?" Everyone has days like that. We've found the best thing on days like that is to take a couple of aspirin and go back to bed.

We think there are no "real," "true," or "second-class" fans, although some folks will try to tell you there are. That's because those folks spend a lot of time researching various aspects of the game, and the label of "real" fan can be an important form of recognition of all of their hard work. Some find joy in accumulating statistics about the 1949 Yankees. Others delve into the evolution of stadium architecture or team uniforms. These hobbies may be fulfilling, but do they mean someone deserves special fan status? We think not. Baseball is just fine without its fans having to create unnecessary pecking orders. Other forms of entertainment seem to thrive without such jostling. After all, symphony regulars usually don't discredit occasional attendees with remarks like, "Mildred! Get this guy behind us. He came to this concert without knowing that Beethoven bridged the classical and romantic periods! The savage!"

So, how about you? Do you enjoy going to a baseball game and eating a hot dog, drinking a cold beer, and feeling the warm sun on your back? Great! Do you enjoy knowing the statistics of the opposing team's pitchers? More power to you! There are fans who like to score entire games and those who want to score only half. There are those who come late and those who leave early—no harm, no foul. We've filled all these roles at one time or another. There are a lot of things going on in a baseball game, and it's any fan's privilege to soak in as little or as much as they please on any given day. Sometimes you'll miss a few of the things happening on the field because you're chatting with your friend during the game. Or perhaps you're digging around in your backpack for a juice box for your kid. Maybe

you're warming up to a new date? And a game may be the perfect place to catch up with your mom. You can tell her you went to Las Vegas last week and eloped. Wow, we hope you are sitting behind us! Game day possibilities are endless!

Whether you choose to be comatose for part of the game or closely involved with every at bat, we hope you'll find this book to be an enjoyable addition to your library. With our treatment of the game's history, stories, strategies, and basic rules, we've tried to write something that will give even the veteran baseball enthusiast a greater understanding of the game. The newer fan—or even someone who's just "baseball curious"—will find this book to be a novel, entertaining, and respectful tool for gaining more appreciation of the game and might learn what all the fuss is about. Read the profiles scattered throughout the book; you'll see some of the many different ways fans have enjoyed the game. And we think there is room for still more incarnations of fandom. Find your niche, and then invite some friends.

This book sometimes tackles what a few fans will find to be arcane baseball ideas and rules. Well, you can't write a baseball book without breaking some eggs. That's what Babe Ruth used to say. OK, you caught us again. But we do try our best to explain some of the more confusing rules. If some points continue to baffle you, re-read them. Still not sure? Send us an e-mail. We may be able to clear things up. Even to some experts, the baseball rulebook looks like an ancient scroll written in Sanskrit.

For the nuts and bolts of the book, we used a number of sources. As expected, our research involved some wonderful baseball books. Then, there was a kind ex-major leaguer who shared his colorful stories. Even Deidre's brother's freakish baseball-card-stats-filled brain proved useful. Throughout the book, we chose different sources in different circumstances for different reasons. The most important thing we learned is to question everything. Especially the stuff we deeply wanted to believe. Through all of that, we still found that relaying accurate statistical information was often a futile undertaking. First, records are a moving target. A player may find himself at the top of a statistical category one year only to be dethroned the next. Second, thanks to those who *do* choose to spend their precious time researching the game's multitudinous particulars, new information about games and players is revealed and regularly updated. Third, it was interesting and often infuriating to see that the game's best-regarded sources

sometimes give conflicting statistical information. For example, some researchers argue convincingly that information on some Hall of Fame plaques is even wrong. So, while researching and writing this book was immensely enjoyable, it sometimes struck us that no one really knew what the heck was going on. So we called and asked to speak to the person in charge. We're still on hold.

Baseball stories have a life of their own. Many are passed down from generation to generation of fans and ballplayers. Not all stories are verifiable, and original sources can't always be found. But that's not the point. Some stories are so good and recited so often that failing to pass them on in this book would be neglectful. While often true, even the unsubstantiated stories are as alive and momentous as the players who once played the game.

And we think the stories from the thousands of people who helped us write this book are equally important. We talked with them while sitting on the grass at spring training games and in the cheap seats at major league ballparks. We befriended them at restaurants and parties and in bathroom lines. The stories don't always revolve around major league players, but they're all legitimate fodder for legends.

You probably already know that baseball is a game, but others who are snooping around in these pages may need to be reminded. Baseball is a game! Some say it reflects life. Let's not take either one too seriously.

Play ball!

SECTION ONE

Baseball, the Musical

In the beginning, there was baseball. And it had two daddies.

Yes, in an awkward misstep, the "Father of Baseball" honor was bestowed upon both Alexander Joy Cartwright and Henry Chadwick. By most accounts, both men were deserving of the title, having handled their historical diaper duties suitably. Alex ran the show on the field. A fireman, bookseller, and bank teller at various times in his early life, he organized the Knickerbockers baseball club in 1845 and is often credited with helping standardize the rules by which today's players abide. Henry, a journalist, was more cerebral. He devised the game's early statistics and popularized baseball through his various rulebooks and guides, first appearing in 1856. It is unlikely that the two men ever met.

For decades, no one questioned the birth of baseball. In fact, few seemed to care about its origin. It wasn't until the early 1900s when people started snooping around that a custody battle ensued.

That's when the Mills Commission, a gaggle of jingoistic baseball gurus, convened to ensure baseball was truly an American invention. At the time, in 1905, nasty rumors swirled that baseball had been adapted from the games of cricket or rounders, both played with some zeal in England. As you might imagine, that would not suffice for America's "national pastime."

The commission found itself in a pickle when there was no credible evidence that baseball didn't evolve from its British cousins. Not to be derailed, commission members freely accepted a quaint tale about how, in 1839, a twenty-year-old military cadet named Abner Doubleday invented baseball in Cooperstown, a rural hamlet in upstate New York. Better yet, Doubleday grew up to be a Civil War officer—a nice bonus for the commission's marketing department. However, having died thirty-four years earlier, Abner was unavailable for comment at the time of his appointment to the position of "inventor of baseball." Plans were soon drawn up to build a museum to honor baseball's rich history. It was to be located in Cooperstown, New York, the, uh, Birthplace of Baseball . . . an inauspicious beginning for the national pastime, indeed.

Vindication came for Cartwright and Chadwick in 1938, when they were inducted as pioneers of the game into baseball's Hall of Fame. These men also had been dead for decades. The following year, the baseball shrine opened to the public to commemorate baseball's centennial, an event based

on when Doubleday had supposedly "invented" the game. There is a nifty baseball field on the grounds of the Hall of Fame called Doubleday Field. And, you now know that the Hall was built in Cooperstown because of the Doubleday legend. But Abner Doubleday, the unwitting interloper, was never enshrined in the Hall of Fame.

Other deserving names were tossed into the "inventor of baseball" ring, some that even cast doubt about the influence of Cartwright and Chadwick. In 1904, Chadwick dismissed the hunt to find the game's true paternity. Taking liberty with a well-worn reference of the time from *Uncle Tom's Cabin*, he said: "Like Topsy, baseball never had no 'fadder,' it jest growed."

Chapter 1

Owners

$\mathscr{I}$t wasn't until almost twenty years after Cartwright laid out the game's earliest set of rules that the first all-salaried team was put together. The Cincinnati Red Stockings were bankrolled in 1869 by local businessmen in the hopes of promoting the city and, of course, pocketing some cash from the endeavor. The ball club was hugely successful. Yet, after spending almost $10,000 in payroll and other expenses, investors split a meager $1.39 profit.

The Reds folded the following year only to regroup in 1876 when the team joined seven other teams in the newly established National League (NL). But, five years later, the team was banished from the league for flouting league rules by serving alcohol at its games and having the audacity to play on Sundays. In 1881, the ball club joined five other teams to form the American Association (AA), a league that welcomed such unrefined behavior.

About 300 miles west, a German immigrant had set up a saloon near St. Louis' Grand Avenue Park. Chris "Vandy" Von der Ahe knew little about sports but quickly learned a few basics from the crowds that gathered to drink beer at his Golden Lion after baseball games. Before long Von der

Ahe boosted his bar's visibility by sponsoring a local, independent baseball club, the St. Louis Brown Stockings. The shrewd marketer set up a beer garden in the stadium, and beer and sporting industries have never looked back.

It seemed divine providence that, along with the Cincinnati Reds, Von der Ahe's Brown Stockings would become one of the six founding members of the American Association. The new league was referred to as the Beer and Whiskey League by sneering fans who preferred the puritanical setting of the National League. Vandy's business sense filled the stadium and fielded winning teams for the ten years of the AA's existence. During the team's most successful years, the Browns were led by their first baseman, player-manager Charlie Comiskey. Fifteen years later, Comiskey became the notoriously stingy owner of the Chicago White Sox, the team forever linked to the shocking baseball scandal of 1919—a failed swindle that you'll read about later in this section.

When the American Association folded in December of 1891, the Browns joined the National League, and things went quickly downhill for Vandy. He plowed through about twenty managers, was kidnapped over an unpaid debt, and saw his baseball stadium engulfed in a vicious fire. By the close of the century, he had been kicked out of the baseball industry altogether.

In 1899 two circling vultures, Frank and Stanley Robison, bought the Browns at auction for $35,000. For much of the 1890s, the Robison brothers operated the competitive Cleveland Spiders, spearheaded by three future hall of famers. Yet attendance dwindled throughout the decade. The hapless St. Louis team, meanwhile, was packing the stadium with a boisterous, beer-swigging bunch. And the Browns held ball games on Sundays—a lucrative prospect that was forbidden within Cleveland's city limits. The Robisons were jealous.

The Robison brothers grew fed up with Cleveland's indifference to the team, and, with only a few days notice, they announced the core Cleveland team would become the St. Louis team; if the players wanted a job, they had to move westward. *Pronto.* To replace the decimated Cleveland franchise, the players for the twelfth-place St. Louis Browns were sent packing to play in Cleveland, where no one seemed to care if the team won or not.

With new faces and a winning spirit in St. Louis, the team became known as the St. Louis "Perfectos," as in "Patsy's Perfectos," in reference to

the team's player-manager and first baseman Patsy Tebeau. The Perfectos went on to a fifth-place finish in 1899 while Cleveland, predictably, finished twelfth.

As baseball evolved through the twentieth century, the game saw all types of owners. Some were hated, loved, racist, enlightened, rich, and poor. For less-wealthy owners like Connie Mack, ownership was a job—like having a paper route. For Gene Autry, the legendary actor who owned a Los Angeles team, ownership was part of enjoying retirement. Like golfing in Palm Springs.

> *From 1986 to '92, during my acting days, I was a waitress and bartender at the Sheraton Grande Hotel in downtown Los Angeles, where many of the teams stayed when playing the Dodgers. I got to know what players were nice to wait on (the players on the Twins and the Padres often traveled with their families) and what players were awful (many of the Mets felt any female was fair game). The morning of a major playoff, I jokingly told several friends that if they had any money, they should bet against the Mets. This is because the major players got so loaded the night before, they would surely be hung over. As I predicted, they lost the game. I wish I had put money on it!*
>
> *—Janet, 48*

CHAPTER 2

Supreme Treatment

$\mathcal{B}$efore there was widespread professional baseball, a grouping of twenty-two amateur teams organized the National Association of Base Ball Players, in 1858. In the span of a decade, the league grew to encompass hundreds of teams across the country. These teams agreed not to accept money for playing and to abide by the same rules that had been mapped out by Alexander Cartwright, who, along with 300,000 other prospectors, traveled west in 1849 to Sierra Nevada as part of the frenzy surrounding the California Gold Rush.

Back east, however, the glow of amateurism was ultimately dampened by the game's success. Fans freely paid admission and players were seduced by experiments with professional baseball in other towns. In fact, some players at the time were covertly bankrolled by businesses, and given jobs and titles that didn't exist. Why not make it official? Indeed, it was during this climate of euphoric capitalism that some teams banded together to create the National Association of *Professional* Base Ball Players. In this incarnation, most of the guys shared a cut of the game day receipts. But the league couldn't assume the toll of having players jump from team to team in search of more money, and it folded in 1876.

Later that year, club owners and other entrepreneurs cheerfully picked up the slack and formed the National League of Professional Base Ball *Clubs*. This is the same National League that Cincinnati joined in 1876, the league's inaugural year, and that the St. Louis Browns joined in 1891, just after the unruly American Association folded. Unlike other baseball leagues of the era, this owner-run league survived and still encompasses half of Major League Baseball (MLB). Some contemporary fans refer to the National League as the "senior circuit" because of its longevity in comparison to the American League (AL), which was established in 1901 and remains the other half of MLB.

But the NL's future seniority was worth nothing at the bank. Looking for a way to turn a profit, owners came up with the "reserve clause" to ensure that players couldn't easily flee to the highest-bidding team, a practice that taxed team payrolls. The clause gave clubs the right to renew the contracts of five players at the end of each season, thereby assuring players of work the following season. Since manual labor was the predominant employment option for young men of that era, chosen players didn't balk when told that they were required to sign a contract to play baseball. It seemed like a plum deal! Certainly preferable to heaving hay on the family farm or chucking coal at the local mill. However, the reserve clause was soon exposed as a slippery slope, and, by the end of the 1880s, owners included a reserve clause in most contracts. Reserving players for the next season gave players no freedom to switch teams or leverage to demand more money. And things got worse.

A landmark 1922 Supreme Court decision in favor of MLB was far-reaching. In this antitrust lawsuit against the league, the high court classified baseball as a "sport" and not a "business." This granted MLB teams immunity from some traditional business laws. The salient implication of the ruling was that the rich owners were organizing just some good, old-fashioned entertainment, and they could do what they pleased, including paying players peanuts if they so desired. The decision essentially rendered the reserve clause impervious to successful legal challenge. Sure, some players mounted protests, but their efforts were discourteously rebuffed.

The best opportunity to break the grip of the reserve clause came in 1970 by way of Curt Flood and the St. Louis Cardinals, which, incidentally, is the same Beer and Whiskey League franchise that Chris Von der Ahe owned ninety years before. A couple years after Vandy was ousted, the team

ditched the "Browns" name and adopted the new "Cardinals" tag that better reflected the team's new uniforms and winning spirit. That was an easy makeover and, by the early 1970s, the team was ready for another. But this time it wouldn't be so effortless, thanks to Flood and his dealings with team owner August Busch, a fat cat from the nearby brewery outfit. (We told you beer and sporting industries never looked back . . .) The animosity between the player and the team's owner culminated in having Flood traded to the Philadelphia Phillies, which Flood was not happy about. First, the team stunk. Second, he deemed the city racist. And many others agreed with him on both counts. After playing with St. Louis for twelve years, he wanted the chance to find another team on his own—perhaps with better pay—instead of being forced to report to the Phillies, which ultimately led to his appeal to become a free agent. But his request was rejected by MLB commissioner Bowie Kuhn. Rather than show up to play baseball in Philadelphia, Flood appealed the ruling in a lawsuit. The court case worked its way all the way to the Supreme Court in *Flood v. Kuhn*.

Fans were aghast that a player who was featured on a *Sports Illustrated* cover and dubbed MLB's best center fielder only two years before would risk his $100,000 annual salary to fight the system solely on principle. But Flood felt the established system was insulting, said that it treated players like a "consignment of goods," and said he, for one, wasn't going to take it anymore. And he didn't. On June 19, 1972, Flood lost his law suit, quit baseball, and spent a few years chilling in Europe. The lifelong smoker battled throat cancer and, in 1997, died at the age of fifty-nine. Two years before his death he granted an interview to a San Francisco reporter. "You know what? I believed in the great American dream," he told her. "I believed if you were right that nine smart men on the Supreme Court would say that. I believed that if you were right, people would understand and be compassionate."

Flood's court battle paved the way for the dissolution of the reserve clause, and for the prevalence of free agency as well as the birth of today's confounding player salaries. But the questionable 1922 Supreme Court antitrust decision remains. This means that major league baseball teams are still granted dispensation from many of the laws that govern other interstate businesses. No other professional sports league, including the National Football League, the National Basketball Association, and the National Hockey League, has this special treatment. The Court admits that

arguments supporting baseball's antitrust exemption are flimsy but puts the onus on Congress to enact laws to change the ruling. This has yet to happen.

Baseball has always been constant in my life; favorite players may switch teams, the stadium changes sponsors more than some players change socks, but the game itself often remains the same. Its complicated simplicity is a beautiful thing. The rhythms, the sounds, the emotions . . . [baseball's] what summer's all about.

—*Jen, 25*

CHAPTER 3

Holding Out for a Hero

Regardless of the reserve clause and the power that baseball owners had, some players were able to bargain for better salaries by simply asking. But often the civilized approach didn't work. When a player didn't like his salary, he could hold out for a suitable offer. Holdouts opt not to play and, consequently, don't get paid. Since there was a plethora of potential players willing to take the place of a holdout—often for less money and certainly for less hassle—owners rarely cared if some disgruntled hack went back to milking goats for a living. Owners took notice, however, when faced with a holdout from a star player. Though management still tried to play hardball, celebrity players often prevailed. Fans paid to see such players and the owners, with an eye toward ticket sales, would sometimes, begrudgingly, entertain salary negotiations.

After two seasons in the majors and a stellar 1908 season, Ty Cobb entered into a bitter contract battle with the owner of the Detroit Tigers. Barbs were tossed at one another through quotes in the press, as they often are today. Finally, despite what Cobb called owner Frank Nevin's "nefarious" behavior during the holdout, the ballplayer accepted a $5,000 salary offer, which was a 100 percent raise. Babe Ruth was another celebrity holdout.

 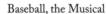

Just months after Black Tuesday and the stock market crash of 1929, the Babe held out for his $80,000. When it was pointed out that he would be earning $5,000 more than President Herbert Hoover, Ruth responded with this famous quote: "Sure, I had a better year than him."

Joe DiMaggio was a precocious negotiator. He started with the Yankees in 1936 earning $8,500; two years later, he was in a contract dispute, demanding $45,000 and ultimately settling for $25,000. During the hold-out, he missed spring training and two weeks of the regular season. In 1942, one year after he set a major league record by amassing fifty-six consecutive games with a hit, DiMaggio refused the Yankees' offer of a $5,000 salary cut. But the Yanks said that they anticipated reduced profits because of World War II and doggedly pursued the pay cut. "Joltin'" Joe ultimately won his money but Yankee management branded him unpatriotic and fans turned their vitriol on him by booing when he came up to bat. His skills at the negotiating table were sharp, though, and by 1949 he bargained a $100,000 contract for that year. Two years later he relinquished his center field position to a strapping young buck, twenty-year-old Mickey Mantle. But DiMaggio didn't wallow in post-baseball pity; a few years after leaving the game, the boy from a poor immigrant neighborhood in San Francisco married starlet Marilyn Monroe and became a half of one of the century's most celebrated and tragic couples.

If a player didn't want to hold out—or didn't have the clout to effectively do so—it was theoretically possible to ask his team to release him from his contract. If the player was any good, a release meant the promise of playing for another team, perhaps for more money. Of course, such releases would create the promise of a free market and soaring player salaries, which no owner wanted. So they simply agreed not to grant such release requests.

In lieu of granting releases, owners traded players for other players, cash, or something of equal value. One such trade set up the fabled "Curse of the Bambino," when Boston Red Sox owner Harry Frazee needed extra cash and unloaded Babe Ruth and his pricey three-year contract just one year after the Babe's pitching helped them win the 1918 World Series. In January of 1920, the New York Yankees snapped up Ruth for $125,000, after which Frazee said the Yankees took a risk on the deal. "The Boston club can now go into the market and buy other players and have a better team . . . [than] if Ruth had remained with us." History shows that few remarks could have been further from the truth. It is speculated that, after paying off his debts, Frazee used the remaining cash to produce the Broadway play *No, No, Nanette,* which opened in 1925. The Yankees went on to win twenty-six World Series titles before the Red Sox fielded their next championship team in 2004.

The practice of trading players is still used and, though modern-day players often get input on where they will be traded, it doesn't work out that way for everyone. In 1992, the Oakland Athletics traded Jose Canseco to the Texas Rangers for three players and cash. When a reporter asked to where Canseco was traded, he responded, "To Ethiopia . . . For a box of Froot Loops and a camel to be named later." All-Star Ruben Sierra, who was traded from Texas in the deal, has not commented on whether he considered himself the camel or among the Froot Loops.

I remember watching the 1980 World Series when I was thirteen years old. My stepfather, Al, would take a shower at the top of the fourth inning of every game. The bathroom he used was right next to the room where my family and our friends would watch each game. Al would have the game on the radio in the bathroom and would bang on the wall whenever the Phillies did something good. The Phillies won the World Series that year—most likely because Al's fourth-inning shower brought them the luck they needed.

—Jennifer, 38

CHAPTER 4

Stuffed Salary

$\mathcal{W}$hile Curt Flood's plight was being reviewed at the Supreme Court, players across the country were becoming antsy with the prospect of free agency. Oakland's "Catfish" Hunter was one of the league's most dominant pitchers in the early 1970s. He had spent ten years with Charlie Finley's Oakland A's and still earned only $100,000, a paltry sum compared to contemporary standards. In 1974, however, things were about to change. After it was determined that Oakland's owner violated Hunter's contract, an arbitrator released the future Hall of Fame pitcher from the agreement—and its reserve clause. This release granted him the right to negotiate a new contract with any team he wanted. This is exactly the same free-agency scenario that Flood fought for a few years earlier. Two weeks after Hunter won his free agency, he signed a five-year, $3.75 million contract with the New York Yankees and owner George Steinbrenner, a shipping magnate who had bought the team two years before.

In 1975, after two other pitchers fought their reserve clauses and won free agency, owners started to scramble and get litigious. Why not? It worked against Curt Flood, after all. However, things had changed. By this point, players were less apt to maintain the code of secrecy regarding salary

negotiations and, as details became known, fans and the media frowned on what looked more like greedy owners not giving players a fare share. The court of public opinion had weighed in; next came the decisions of jurors and arbitrators, who were less inclined to help the owners maintain the status quo. Defeated, owners reluctantly accepted a new order. This effectively ended the power of the reserve clause and opened the door for rampant free agency.

The growing prevalence of free agency led superstars to negotiate big contracts in the late '70s. Soon, owners were pushed to come up with clever ways to keep profits in line. One solution was to have all the owners refuse to sign any free agents, surmising that, with a lack of demand for free agents, salaries would fall. The plan worked. In 1987, average player salaries dropped for the first time since the dawn of all this free agency business. The owners had cheated the system and were getting away with it. Well, that was until they got busted. Players were granted a settlement to compensate for the illegal collusion on the part of the owners, and the two parties went back to their war rooms to plot the next attack.

And assault, they did. For the next fifteen years, baseball was wracked with labor pains that resulted in a battery of threats, strikes by the ballplayers, a lockout by the owners, and, in 1994, a cancelled World Series. Through all of this, though, salaries plodded upwards. By 2008, the lowest salary was $390,000, and the year's average salary swelled past $3 million.

Major League Baseball's attitude change about free agency was due partly to pressure from the public and Congress, since Congress was—and still is—the keeper of the antitrust exemption granted by the 1922 Supreme Court decision. And with that power, Congress had MLB by the equipment bag. In the name of social justice, Congress appears to use the threat of removing the league's antitrust exemption as a cudgel to get MLB to act on things Americans find important. This was seen when league executives and players were dragged in front of a Congressional hearing in 2005. The hearings were an effort to force the league to amend its superficial drug-testing policy. But much of what the public remembers from those hearings is the tearful testimony from a mortal-sized Mark McGwire, who flatly refused to answer questions about his suspected steroid abuse during his bloated playing days. And who can forget the arrogant finger-wagging from Rafael Palmeiro, a respected active player, while claiming that he didn't use steroids, either. And many of us actually believed him. The blinding light

from those hearings brought the league's widespread steroid abuse from clubhouse winks and nods into our living rooms and dinner conversations.

A year after the congressional hearings, baseball commissioner Bud Selig tasked former senator George Mitchell with following up on a decade's worth of accusations and accounts from players, trainers, and clubhouse "assistants" about performance-enhancing drug use in MLB. In December 2007, the investigation's findings were released in the "Mitchell report," which implicated some of baseball's biggest stars. This sent players into a flurry of everything from denial to silence. Yankee pitcher Roger Clemens, a sure-fire Hall of Famer, used the former tactic when he publicly lashed out against his trainer's damaging testimony. Clemens said in a TV interview that the things reported "never happened." Immediate fallout from the report also included a Rose Garden rebuke about steroid abuse from President George Bush, who was flanked by members of Congress, to Major League Baseball. All of this left much of the public with the uncomfortable feeling that nothing could ever be solved when it comes to unveiling the story behind performance-enhancing drugs in baseball. Worse was that, perhaps, it didn't matter anymore. But some of those in Congress seemed to care, even if it was under the auspices of patrolling the antitrust perimeter.

Many fans find it somewhat unbelievable that the special exemption marches on. As for MLB, it took the league twenty years to amend its rulebook to allow officially for player free agency. The new rule is referred to as the "Curt Flood Act of 1998."

I'm an Oakland girl who grew up going to baseball games. I like everything about [baseball]. When I was nine years old, I went with my dad to see Catfish Hunter, Vida Blue, Reggie Jackson. . . . I caught a couple of balls as a kid and kept autographed balls for years. I'm now a grandmother and my dear ol' dad is 97. We still go to the games together. So what do I like about the game? Everything!

—Jowhari, 48

## CHAPTER 5

Changes in the Air

With all due respect to various branches of government, baseball is a business, and, as such, money-making schemes are as old as the game. This is a story about simple economics: as the game became more popular, tempting opportunities emerged for earning more money. Concessions finally became available for attendees in the late 1800s. That's about forty years of baseball without a hotdog and a beer! Today's gourmet offerings such as garlic fries, pepperoni pizza, and buffalo wings are a direct result of what fans said they wanted. How did it all come to pass? It didn't happen overnight. Rather, the game has followed a somewhat logical, though occasionally inane, path to the garishness that some modern fans find so offensive.

Thumbing through Great Aunt Julia's vintage baseball card collection, we were transported back to the early days of baseball, back to the tattered and faded black-and-white photos of players like Ty Cobb and Honus Wagner. And the technicolor line drawing of a Pee Wee Reese baseball card. Sure, the game was different then. Before the gargantuan contracts and the ensuing disputes, didn't these guys honestly play for sheer enjoyment? Maybe. The Gilded Age of baseball, if it ever existed, didn't last long. From its infancy, moneyed owners and salaried players drew the ire of fans.

Songwriter H.C. Dodge was one such disappointed fan. Normally busy writing scathing political verse, Dodge was so bothered by what had become of the national pastime, he penned these lines in 1886:

Oh, don't you remember the game of base-ball we saw twenty years ago played,

When contests were true, and the sight free to all, and home-runs in plenty were made?

When we lay on the grass, and with thrills of delight, watched the ball squarely pitched at the bat,

And easily hit, and then mount out of sight along with our cheers and our hat?

And then, while the fielders raced after the ball, the men on the bases flew round,

And came in together—four batters in all. Ah! That was the old game renowned.

Now salaried pitchers, who throw the ball curved at padded and masked catchers,

And gate-money music and seats all reserved is all that is left of the game.

Oh, give us the glorious matches of old, when love of true sport made them great,

And not this new-fashioned affair always sold for the boodle they take at the gate.

Chances are Dodge didn't renew his season-ticket package.

Various professional baseball leagues spent the latter part of the 1800s adding teams, dropping teams, experimenting with rules, and generally hammering out details that would, undoubtedly, be abominable to Dodge and others who considered themselves among the game's traditionalists. But by the beginning of the 1900s, the game had settled into a format that would stand unchanged for five decades. Major League Baseball consisted of sixteen teams in 1903, eight in both the AL and the NL. Five cities accounted for eleven of the total, which meant the game was represented in only ten cities. Perhaps calling the game the "national" pastime

was a bit of a misnomer? Well, regardless, the game covered some of the country's large population centers. New York City had three teams; Boston, Philadelphia, Chicago, and St. Louis each had two. Unlike today, teams in different leagues didn't play against each other. In fact, many National League players considered themselves and their league more professional than the newly formed American League and those who played in it.

Despite the acrimony between the leagues, the owner of the NL-winning Pittsburgh Pirates wrote a letter near the end of the 1903 season to the owner of the Boston Pilgrims, (which later became known as the Red Sox) whose team had the best record in the AL. This letter suggested that the two leagues organize a World Series, an annual series of games during which the best team in the AL would oppose the best team in the NL. The two owners were looking to boost interest in baseball and figured that creating a "world" championship would be a solid long-term financial investment.

The first World Series was played that year between the Pirates and the Pilgrims. Boston won the best-of-nine-games series, five games to three. And the event was a big boodle-maker! But the following year's World Series hit a snag when the New York Giants, the NL winners, refused to play in the World Series. This was because they thought that the Boston team, and the entire AL in general, was not worthy of the contest. So there was no World Series in 1904, making it one of only two years since 1903 that the World Series hasn't been played.

With the kinks in the World Series worked out, including changing the format to a best-of-seven series, baseball hit a comfortable stride. That was until March 1953. That year, the Boston Braves moved to Milwaukee. The Braves franchise had been in New England for seventy-seven years but stayed in Milwaukee for only thirteen years before moving to Atlanta, where the team has remained. And, after the 1953 season, the St. Louis Browns moved to the Atlantic seaboard to become the Baltimore Orioles. (Chris Von der Ahe's St. Louis franchise, which was named the "Browns" before the Robison brothers took over, stayed along the banks of the Mississippi River, where the team, the Cardinals, remains.) In 1955, the Philadelphia Athletics stopped in Kansas City for twelve years before finally landing in Oakland. The West Coast settlements were pioneered in 1958 by the relocated New York Giants and Brooklyn Dodgers, who moved to San Francisco and Los Angeles, respectively.

Walter O'Malley, the Dodgers' owner, was particularly skewered for moving his team. Fans and newspaper reporters branded the exodus a greedy and sneaky act. They argued that it was a betrayal to take the team away from its fans. And history has been less kind. But O'Malley, for his part, was frustrated looking for a suitable Brooklyn site to build a spiffy, larger Dodger stadium. The team had played in Ebbets Field since 1913, and the facility was cramped and decrepit. It was a swath of land perfect for a new stadium that lured O'Malley to Los Angeles. When he got there, what he found was a giant headache.

O'Malley arrived in Los Angeles in January of 1958 and found the stadium building process mired in legal entanglements. The site of the proposed stadium was a political battleground known as Chavez Ravine, a large Mexican community that had thrived for generations. City officials ordered much of the three-hundred-acre site bulldozed in 1950 to make way for a controversial public housing project called Elysian Park Heights. The bickering eventually landed the housing plans in the shredder, and O'Malley purchased the land as a site for his ballpark. Citizen opposition to having the public land used for a private business was virulent, but it wasn't insurmountable. Los Angeles politicians ushered the stadium plan through the system and cleared out the stragglers still living in Chavez Ravine. During the three-year period of debate and stadium construction, O'Malley's team played in the thirty-five-year-old Los Angeles Memorial Coliseum. On April 10, 1962, the Dodgers played their first game in the new stadium in front of 52,564 fans and lost to Cincinnati, 6-3.

By the time the new Dodger stadium was built, there was already a new act in town. In 1961, Gene Autry, a Hollywood screen legend known as the "Singing Cowboy," fielded a second team in Southern California, the Los Angeles Angels, an AL team, and MLB continued to expand, just as any business would. By 1969, there were twenty-four teams, total—twelve in each league. Both the AL and the NL broke up their teams evenly into East and West divisions. When O'Malley's Dodgers arrived in L.A. for the 1958 season, the team was one of eight NL teams, and by the end of the 1960s, the team played in the six-team NL West division.

While the MLB business grew, other changes were afoot. Teams in the 1950s battled television's hypnotic command over the game's new, suburban fan base. Owners started to realize how media revenue could affect a team's bottom line and began granting rights to a radio or television station

to broadcast games. Back in the 1930s, the three New York teams forbade live radio broadcasts of their games because owners worried that the transmissions would lead to decreased attendance. But teams eventually gave in, only to question the decision later. "We found that our increase in TV revenue was in direct proportion to our decline in attendance," O'Malley told *TV Guide* in 1975. Before long, the prospect of money from media companies became the tail that wagged the dog. More night games were scheduled to capitalize on the viewership of stay-at-home fans, and teams signed radio and television contracts worth hundreds of millions of dollars a year.

Changes to the playoff structure, which had stood unchanged since 1903, were also on the horizon. This was driven by expansion and the addition of divisions in each league. A 1969 update pitted the two East and West division winners in each league against each other in a best-of-five playoff. The team that emerged from that series would be awarded the league pennant and would play for the World Series championship title against the winner from the other league. So, post-1969, fans in four cities gathered around their television sets to follow their team into the postseason; including the World Series, they would watch as many as seventeen televised playoff games. Indeed, owners no longer questioned the decision to take TV revenue. But wait, there's more! The promise of added income was such that, in 1985, the division playoffs were changed to a best-of-seven series. Oh boy.

By 1995 MLB had expanded again, creating a "Central" division in both leagues. A few more teams were added since then, making fifteen teams in each league that are split—not necessarily evenly, as logic might suggest—among the East, Central, and West divisions. Because scheduling a pennant playoff series between three division winners was impossible, MLB created a "wild card" team for both the NL and AL. The wild card goes to the team that has the best record among the second place teams across its league's three divisions. The wild card makes it so that four teams (three division winners and one wild card winner) face off in two best-of-five divisional playoffs in each league. Usually, the wild card team plays the team with the best record in the league in one division playoff while the other two teams play in the other divisional series, unless the wild card team and the first-place team are in the same division. Then they mix it up so two teams from the same division don't play one another. Did we just see you roll your eyes? We feel your pain. We, too, would like to find the guy who dreamed up this scheme.

When the two division winners in each league are decided, they play a best-of-seven-games series for the league pennant. This set of playoff games is called the league championship series, and there's one for both leagues (NLCS and ALCS). The winner of each league's championship series carries its pennant to the World Series. Upon arriving, the teams play for pride, cash, and, since the 1920s, a ring for everyone on the team. We should point out that said ring has seemingly become more gaudy with each passing media contract and product endorsement deal. And, if you would, venture back with us to the conversation about TV revenues. Oh, and grab your calculator. That is because today's devoted fans are held hostage for the better part of October as the drama of a possible forty-one postseason baseball games unfold on television. Carry the one . . . and don't forget the dollar sign. Yep, that's a huge number.

After toying around with the postseason and television contracts, the powers that be still weren't satisfied. So, in an effort to boost interest in the game, the league instituted interleague play. This meant that NL teams would play AL teams during the regular season. Before 1997, the only time a NL team would meet an AL team in an official game would be in the postseason World Series. Was the commissioner of baseball out of his tree? Many fans thought so; to them, the move to have teams play out of their league was an abomination, a slap in the face to the Father of Baseball . . . whoever that might be.

My mom and dad came to visit me in San Francisco, and we went to Sunday Mass, which happened to be the first Mass for a new priest, Father Xavier Lavagetto. At one point, they said a prayer for Fr. Xavier's father, Cookie. Well, my father's eyes lit up and he acted like a young boy. After Mass, he introduced himself to Mrs. Lavagetto and shared a story of how how he stayed to watch Cookie during a very close Dodgers game and was late meeting his mother because of it. Cookie was one of his favorite players and here he was talking to his wife! I had never seen my father get so nervous and excited about meeting someone before.

—Margaret, 41

Chapter 6

Branching Out

*I*n the early days of the game, blacks and whites occasionally played organized baseball together. This was either on the same team or, more often, on opposite teams. And that system seemed to work. But near the end of the 1800s, owners stopped signing black players to their mostly white teams. This created the need for separate playing circuits, which continued to exist for about sixty years. The separation of players came to an end when MLB owners and managers could no longer ignore the abundance of tremendously talented black players.

The decades of segregated leagues meant that some of the game's iconic players—black and white—tragically never faced the full spectrum of talented baseball players. White superstars like Ty Cobb, Babe Ruth, and Lou Gehrig never played against their black counterparts in the Negro Leagues. The better part of Joe DiMaggio's career, which ended in 1951, occurred before blacks and whites played on the same field. One such gifted black player was Josh Gibson. A looming presence at the plate, he was known as the "Black Babe Ruth" and was considered one of the best power hitters to ever play the game. Gibson was consigned, however, to the Negro Leagues for his entire career, which spanned from 1930 to 1946. Other

greats who spent their entire professional careers in the Negro Leagues were Buck Leonard and Cool Papa Bell, both teammates of Gibson's when they played with the ten-time champion Homestead Grays. Satchel Paige made the move from the Negro Leagues to the major leagues in 1948 at about the age of forty two, when he was drafted to play for the Cleveland Indians. Not surprisingly, Paige had hit his prime about twenty years before—right around the same time Lou Gehrig's major league career was starting to heat up. In 1927, for example, while Paige was tearing up the Negro Leagues, Gehrig won his first of two Most Valuable Player (MVP) awards. Yet these two superstars never played against each other. Similarly, the big-swinging Gibson never had to face Lefty Grove, a pitching powerhouse who played for the all-white New York Yankees during Gibson's remarkable Negro League career.

After World War II, sports were fully integrated in many college, semipro, and international leagues, and the public became vocal about the glaring omission of blacks in MLB, especially after many had been sent to war to fight fascism abroad. A protest sign outside of Yankee Stadium read, "If we are able to stop bullets, why not balls?" In fact, the major leagues were among the last bastions of segregation in baseball. Branch Rickey, the general manager of the Brooklyn Dodgers, thought the time was ripe to act. He conquered the league's scorn of black players when he lured Jackie Robinson away from the Kansas City Monarchs, a Negro League team, to play for his Dodgers franchise.

Having considered integration for many years, Rickey was aware of the obstacles toward bringing black players to the major leagues—most notably, baseball's commissioner Kenesaw Mountain Landis. But Rickey, having spent thousands of dollars scouting the Negro Leagues for the right player to test the waters, was patient. Less than a year after Landis died, Rickey tapped Jackie Robinson for his unmatched skill, unflappable demeanor, and fortitude. Conveniently, as many black men during this time were shunned—or hanged—for dating white women, Robinson was in a tidy relationship with a black woman, Rachel Isum, whom he married in 1946.

A story tells how, in an exchange between Rickey and Robinson in 1945, the general manager mimicked the abuse expected from white fans by shouting racial slurs into the ball player's face to see how he would react. "Mr. Rickey, do you want a player who doesn't have the guts to fight back?"

Robinson asked. "No, I want a player with the guts *not* to fight back," Rickey replied.

Jackie Robinson was twenty-eight when he was "called up" from the minor leagues to play for the 1947 Brooklyn Dodgers. Though more black players slowly followed, it was not a welcoming environment. It is speculated that some umpires had larger strike zones for black than they did for white players. Often black players were taunted by fans and scorned by teammates. On road trips, black players slept in separate hotels and ate in separate restaurants from their white teammates. In the late 1950s, Vic Power, a black major league infielder born in Puerto Rico, was told by a waitress in Little Rock, Arkansas, that the restaurant didn't serve blacks. He handled this with his usual charm: "That's okay," he replied, "I don't eat them."

The year that Robinson first appeared in the major leagues, an editorial in the *Sporting News* blasted the idea of integration, accusing teams of "forcing" blacks into the big leagues so that owners could get fat on the profits and exposure. Indeed, owners who integrated were handsomely rewarded, and money, recognition, and championships followed. In 1947, Jackie Robinson won the league's first Rookie of the Year award and led his Brooklyn Dodgers team to the World Series. The following season, Larry Doby and Satchel Paige were the first black players to win a World Series when their Cleveland Indians, under the ownership of showman Bill Veeck, beat the Boston Braves. Meanwhile, the most prominent black baseball leagues suffered the loss of their star players and soon folded. This downfall was also a financial hit to the Major League teams that rented their stadiums to local Negro League teams when the stadium was not in use by the MLB team. Clearly, for some major league ballclubs, segregation was good for business.

History shows that many of MLB's first black players were not only the impetus for greatness, as can be seen in leading teams to championships, but many of these guys were also simply great. For most of the decade following Robinson's first game, baseball's MVP awards for the National League went overwhelmingly to black players. Robinson won it in 1949, and Roy Campenella, who joined the Dodgers in 1948, was MVP in 1951, 1953, and 1955. The New York Giants' Willie Mays won the award in 1954, and pitcher Don Newcombe, another Dodger, not only won MVP in 1956, but, that same year, was the first player to win the Cy Young award, pitching's

most prestigious honor. Milwaukee's Hank Aaron was MVP in 1957, and Ernie Banks, a shortstop for the Cubs known as "Mr. Cub," won it in 1958 and 1959. The American League was slower to integrate. In 1959, three years after Robinon retired from baseball, the AL's Boston Red Sox added Pumpsie Green to its roster, making it the last team to integrate. And the Yankee's Elston Howard was the AL's first black MVP, winning the award in 1963.

The prospect of earning money from these talented black players had tantalized major league teams almost as soon as the decision was made in the early 1900s not to allow blacks to play. The early years of baseball holds several stories about how owners tried to sneak players of "questionable ethnicity" onto team rosters, with varying success. Some of these players were Cuban, American Indian, or from the Dominican Republic. In 1901, John McGraw, Baltimore's player-manager, introduced the world to a Cherokee Indian named "Chief Tokohama." It was soon found out that the Chief was really a light-skinned black second baseman named Charlie Grant and a star for his Negro League team, the Columbia Giants. "Somebody said this Cherokee of McGraw's is really Grant, the crack Negro second baseman, fixed up with war paint and a bunch of feathers," said Charlie Comiskey, owner of the Chicago White Sox. "If Mugsy [McGraw] really keeps this Indian, I will get a Chinaman of my acquaintance and put him on third. Probably I might whitewash a colored man."

I think that football and basketball are more difficult to watch, with the crowding and piling up of bodies. Baseball, unlike other sports, also has a tremendous sense of history—a history of stats and records. The stats place you in a certain time and somehow indicate the broader (non-baseball) historical context in which they occurred. For example, the amazing summer of '41 on the eve of World War II.

—Erin, 35

CHAPTER 7

All-Star Game

$\mathcal{I}$t's fun to think that major league players started out as scrawny little kids dreaming about one day donning a major league uniform. Playing alone in their backyards sometimes, they would toss the ball up in the air and swing away!—picturing the game winning home run that wins the World Series. Or, growing up to be so respected by fans that they are chosen to be on an All-Star team.

Aw, aren't kids cute?

All-Star players gather to play in MLB's annual All-Star Game, an exhibition match-up between the best National League and American League players. Each league's team is assigned a manager, a role filled by the manager of the team who played at the previous World Series. Fans vote for the starting lineup and pitchers; the "reserves," or non-starters, are selected by the All-Star team managers. Additionally, each MLB team must be represented on its league's roster. This means that if the fans don't cover all of the ballclubs with their starting picks, which happens often, the All-Star manager has to cover any team omissions among those he picks for reserves. The All-Star Game is often referred to as the Midsummer Classic because it's played in early July. For the majority of MLB players,

however, it is more like the All-Star "break," because those who aren't picked to play on their league's team get to relax for a few days.

The first All-Star Game was intended to be the only one of its kind but was so lucrative that it became a summer tradition. The Chicago White Sox hosted the exhibition event in Comiskey Park in 1933. The game featured future Hall of Famers Babe Ruth and Lou Gehrig. Ruth knocked a two-run homer over the outfield fence to lead the American League to a 4-2 win. And, much like today, some players were star-struck. "We wanted to see the Babe," said St. Louis' Wild Bill Hallahan, who was pitching for the National League. "Sure, he was old and had a big waistline, but that didn't make any difference. We were on the same field as Babe Ruth."

Aw, aren't thirty-year-old baseball players cute?

Indeed, but some of them aren't as cute as others. For example, after the fans show their adoration with their votes, some of the starters refuse to show up, opting instead to take the three-day hiatus to relax or nurse an aching body. Would a broken nose qualify as an ache? Not according to Orioles' shortstop Cal Ripken, who played six innings of the 1996 All-Star Game with a tweaked beak held together with gauze. (Now, *that's* cute!) Then there are those players who show up, only to duck out early. *Sports Illustrated* reported that Alex Rodriguez confessed that he once played in the beginning of an All-Star Game and headed home to watch the end of it on his couch. Our proprietary research says that the game was in Milwaukee. His couch was in Miami. You do the math.

While the All-Star Game is considered one of the most popular in American sports, it has lost some of its allure over the years. This may have to do with the fact that many fans can see these players whenever they want on TV. That luxury was non-existent or rare for fans until the 1980s, when cable stations started airing a multitude of weekly games. Additionally, the prevalence of interleague games means that celebrated players from the other leagues may play a few games in the local stadium. This was impossible before interleague play was introduced in 1997. And for the twenty-five years after the first All-Star Game in Chicago, there were no teams west of St. Louis. Many fans in the western states had never seen a major league ballgame played at all. Fans would flock to All-Star Games to see some of the game's heroes, players that they connected with only through occasional newspaper accounts or radio broadcasts.

The game has recently had a string of public relations hits, starting in 1993 when Baltimore's pitcher Mike Mussina instigated a change in the event format by, from what some say, acting like a spoiled brat. In his second All-Star Game, the young Mussina was likely excited to play the Midsummer Classic in his home stadium, Baltimore's Oriole Park at Camden Yards. Near the end of the game, he made an executive decision to start warming up, and it looked as if he were going to pitch in the game. This riled up the Baltimore crowd because they thought that they would get to see him play. But the manager never put him in the game and never instructed him to warm up. When the game ended and Mussina hadn't made an appearance, fans revolted. The ensuing fuss went all the way up to MLB executives. After that point All-Star managers were pressured to play everyone on their rosters. The new plan had a ripple effect that made some fans think that staging an interesting and competitive game was less important to MLB than soothing players' fragile egos or appealing to a player's mom, who is sitting in the stands hoping to see her little pumpkin play.

And now managers have to worry about what to do if an All-Star Game becomes a dramatic, extra-inning contest, because they have to budget their players so that everyone has a chance to play during a regulation nine-inning game. If the game goes into extra innings, he may run out of players, or the guys who happen to be playing at the end of the ninth inning might have to keep playing until the game is finished, regardless of how long it lasts.

This concern was brought to the forefront during the 2002 All-Star Game at Milwaukee's Miller Park. The game was tied up in the eleventh inning and was fixing to be one of the most exciting All-Star Games in ages, until both teams ran out of pitchers. This can happen in All-Star Games when managers substitute players early and often because they are reluctant to tax a player too much, possibly rendering him fragile, tired, or hurt for the rest of his season. While it is true that some managers are accused of—are *famous* for—overusing players in regular season games, doing so in the All-Star exhibition game is unacceptable. Seeing the conundrum during the 2002 All-Star Game, commissioner Bud Selig intervened in the eleventh inning, calling the game a 7-7 tie. Afterward, fans threw bottles and chanted "refund" in protest. Another fan held up a sign that read "There are only ties in hockey."

The truncated 2002 All-Star Game was widely recognized as a debacle. It was also emblematic of the kind of debates that rage in baseball. Fans suggested, and with some good evidence, that the All-Star Game didn't really matter to MLB as much as it mattered to them. See, there were more than 40,000 people jammed into Miller Park that day. This game was important to many of those fans—and, perhaps especially important to those who took off work and paid to fly to Milwaukee, stay in hotels, and eat in restaurants for the three-day All-Star break.

Selig responded with an initiative to show fans that the outcome of the All-Star Game was relevant, awarding the winning league home-field advantage for the upcoming World Series. Playing in a home stadium has many perks. One advantage is that, if the World Series goes to seven games, the pivotal game is played in the stadium of the team with home-field advantage, forcing the visiting teams to shoulder the fans' booing and taunts. By making this benefit hinge on the result of the All-Star Game, Selig appeased skeptical fans. Maybe home-field advantage would carry enough weight so that the best players would show up and play. But urging All-Star managers to include every player on the roster, as opposed to fielding the best team for the entire game, compromises Selig's best intentions in this regard. It seems like the league was trying to serve two masters and found the pursuit dicey. This is especially true when one of the masters is a proud mother with a camcorder.

Many players can become All-Stars, and the range of talent among them is vast. Some players make an appearance only once in their careers, such as the token representative to an otherwise overlooked team. Other players are selected by fans year after year. This even can be after the player has long passed his prime as an athlete. In fact, because of this practice, many fans deride the All-Star Game as an outdated popularity contest. However, the votes for craggy, veteran players can be seen as a show of respect for a solid career, one that may even make a player worthy of induction into the Hall of Fame.

I remember listening to an Orioles game on a very hot afternoon in 1982 and realizing that, oh my God, they might make the playoffs! I jumped in the car and drove to the stadium while the game was still on to get the tickets for the next day's final season game. But the playoffs went down the tubes when Palmer lost the final game 10-2. But that's the game, isn't it? And that's Palmer.

—*Dottie, 95*

CHAPTER 8

Hall of Immortality

The Hall of Fame was built to serve as a museum to baseball's great legacy and great players. It was also built to lure tourists to tiny Cooperstown and to make money for the town and MLB. But, since this is a long book, we'll drop the overt cynicism—for now. In 1936, Ty Cobb, Babe Ruth, Christy Mathewson, Walter Johnson, and Honus Wagner were the first players inducted into the Baseball Hall of Fame.

Though there have been a few exceptions and various changes over the years, getting voted into the Hall of Fame is much like trying out for a high school team. Everyone knows the guys who will be starters for the Varsity squad. Other kids battle for a place on the Varsity team, yet still spend some games watching from the dugout while some punk gets a shot at his position. Then there are the guys who get sent down to Junior Varsity, some who carry a grudge at their lesser status, some who are just happy that they get the chance to play at all, and still more who never do get to play. The Hall's induction process can be about as frustrating and pitiful as watching kids get cut from that high school team. To be sure, the road to Cooperstown is lined with the carcasses of great players spurned.

A player is eligible for the Hall of Fame after he has spent five years in retirement following a major-league career that spanned a minimum of ten years. This means that a new crop of retirees becomes eligible for the Hall of Fame ballot every year. And, every year, a special committee of baseball writers nominates players from this new class of eligible former players, ultimately deciding which players get to play the Hall of Fame game. If a player doesn't get chosen to be on the ballot the first year he becomes eligible for it, his chance with the baseball writers has passed him by. Each baseball writer then votes for up to ten of the players on the ballot, which is comprised of the new guys and other players who received at least 5 percent of the previous year's Hall of Fame vote. Because the 5 percent benchmark signifies some measured, though marginal, interest in the player, the system offers multiple chances—up to fifteen years on the ballot—for players to get inducted. If the player can't muster up 5 percent of the vote, his name is removed from future ballots. Many players, like Ozzie Guillen, who in 2005 managed the Chicago White Sox to its first World Series Championship since 1917, get booted after the first year on the ballot. Other players hang around the Hall of Fame ballot like a jilted boyfriend, hoping someone will convince the ex that he is really a great catch. Before long these players can't get even 5 percent of the vote and are dropped from the ballot. Or, worse, he could exist like Dave Concepcion who hung around on the ballot for fifteen years, ending with the 2008 vote. The year before, the same fate befell Steve Garvey. The ten-time All-Star first baseman and 1974 MVP never cracked the 43 percent mark. Interest in him was never marginal during those fifteen years, though; it was passionate and newsworthy. But it wasn't enough.

The 2007 vote was highly anticipated. About 550 writers received a ballot with the names of thirty-two former players. Along with older names such as Garvey and Red Sox slugger Jim Rice, the ballot included new guys like Tony Gwynn and Cal Ripken, Jr., who were the sure varsity starters. Thus, the excitement wasn't based on whether Gwynn and Ripken would get into the Hall of Fame, but, rather, by what percentage. There was also interest around whether Garvey and Rice would finally get voted in. As it so happened, Ripken and Gwynn were the only two on that year's ballot to get at least 75 percent of the total votes, which is the necessary popularity level to be inducted into Cooperstown. Baseball writers that year spared Harold Baines, who received just over 5 percent of the vote in his first year

on the ballot. But Orel Hersiser's twenty-four votes garnered only 4 percent of the total in his second year on the ballot (down from 11 percent in 2006). Hershisher was in good company that year, though, as he was one of the fifteen players booted off subsequent years' ballots because they all missed the minimum 5 percent mark in 2007. Picture the bloodshed! No one has ever been voted in unanimously, though Tom Seaver, a pitcher with a twenty-year MLB career, came close; he scored nearly ninety-nine percent of the votes his first year of eligibility.

As of early 2008, there were 199 former major league players voted into the Hall of Fame. This includes thirty-eight "first ballot" guys who, like Seaver, Gwynn, and Ripken were voted in as soon as they became eligible. Being selected on the first ballot is a distinction held by only the greatest players. Certain players are even referred to as first ballot Hall of Famers while still active major league players. One example is pitching legend Roger Clemens, who played for four teams during his twenty-four-year career. The discussion about his imminent induction has included such seemingly trivial topics as which team's hat Hall of Fame officers will have him don for the ceremony. But the hat issue is not a trifling affair to Clemens, who in 2003 told reporters that he wanted to wear a Yankees hat. "I play twenty years, work my tail off, they're not going to tell me what hat I'm wearing, I promise you that . . . There might be a vacant seat there. I'll take my mother, and we'll go to Palm Springs and invite all y'all, and we'll have our own celebration."

Well, if Clemens can successfully dodge the negative publicity stemming from the Mitchell report, his commanding career really does make the vote a formality. Aside from his dominance for most of his career, Clemens has the requisite pitching achievement that, historically, precedes a call from Cooperstown. Every pitcher who amassed 300 wins during the course of a career has been invited to join the other baseball immortals. On June 13, 2003, Clemens reached this mark when his Yankees beat the St. Louis Cardinals, 5-2.

There are certain other benchmark statistics that have historically guaranteed near-automatic induction into the Hall. So far, every eligible player who has accumulated 3,000 hits or 500 home runs gets a call. However, as the game continues to change, the voting mass may have a few things with which to grapple. One is that certain statistics have new meaning in a new era. For example, for many years only the most feared power hitters

of a generation were capable of hitting 500 home runs in a career. But the bicep-bulging steroid scandal of the late 1990s changed all that, making it seem as though the benchmark was attainable by pretty average players. That would be someone like Jose Canseco, who retired after getting rich off of his 462 career homers and then got richer writing a tell-all book about steroids in MLB. And during Mark McGwire's home run tear that ultimately garnered him 583 career home runs, the press plastered his name across headlines and his picture on front pages. His image was that of a gracious and kind gentle giant. But now, baseball writers have yet to grant him passage into the Hall of Fame. Very public is the impression that McGwire was not voted into the Hall because of unsubstantiated though compelling accusations that steroids may have helped him hit some of those homers. These are the same rumors, incidentally, that much of the press didn't stubbornly pursue during McGwire's playing years. And now they judge—harshly. Players such as Rafael Palmeiro and Barry Bonds also broke the once-revered 500-homer barrier. However, the specter of performance-enhancing drugs has brought new scrutiny to their numbers, as well.

In the past, Hall of Fame voters have inducted every eligible player who's amassed at least 3,000 hits during the course of his career. As of 2008, three "retirees" in the 3,000 Club are waiting to see if they will make it to Cooperstown. Rickey Henderson, who finished his major league career with 3,055 hits, will be eligible for the Hall of Fame in 2009. A few years after Henderson's likely first-ballot election to Cooperstown, Palmeiro and Craig Biggio will see if they make the cut. Pete Rose retired from his spectacular playing career in 1986 with 4,256 hits—the most ever by any major leaguer. Rose, however, was banned from baseball for life because of a gambling scandal in 1989, when it was revealed that he bet on the Cincinnati Reds while he was the team's manager. After rounds of legal wrestling, Rose was dealt a final blow a few years later when it was decided that those banned from baseball were also ineligible for the Hall of Fame. The league officials deemed Rose's offense unforgivable, and this was a fate for which he was unprepared. Had all gone according to destiny, Rose would have been a first-ballot Hall of Famer in 1992. But his name never appeared on the ballot, which didn't deter some voters. Rose got forty-one protest votes that year, all write-ins. It was the same year that Tom Seaver was a first-ballot inductee.

Perhaps Rose was treated so harshly because his transgression was considered akin to the Black Sox disaster of 1919. That year, eight players of the Chicago White Sox, owned by Charlie Comiskey, a miserly fellow, were found guilty of taking money to lose that year's World Series to the Cincinnati Reds. All eight players were banned from baseball, including "Shoeless" Joe Jackson, an illiterate whose name was tied to the scam. His questionable involvement and his otherwise assured Hall of Fame status make Jackson one of the most enduring and heartbreaking figures associated with the scandal.

When a player is passed over after he's been on the ballot for fifteen years, he can be reconsidered by the Veterans Committee, which includes all living Hall of Famers. It is possible that, if the fervor over his treason ever subsides, Pete Rose could even be voted in posthumously. He's banned from baseball for life, after all, not for eternity. Ditto for Shoeless, who died in 1951. But while the Veterans Committee can be seen as a second chance for players who baseball writers didn't deem worthy, it has also drawn criticism. Charged with inducting managers, executives, and umpires, the committee's 2008 Hall of Fame inductions stunned reporters and fans. The ire originated from the selection of Walter O'Malley, the owner detested for shunning a loyal fanbase and moving his Brooklyn team to Los Angeles, and Bowie Kuhn, Curt Flood's backward-thinking rival in his bid to become a free agent. What makes Kuhn's induction all the more bothersome to some is that the committee rejected the contributions of his nemesis, Marvin Miller, the man who helped organize the players into a union. Miller's involvement forced baseball to change while Kuhn fought it. Yet, look who is immortalized.

By the time Ted Williams was inducted to the Hall in 1966, Jackie Robinson was the only black player included in the elite club. Williams used the pulpit of his induction speech to ask that Negro Leaguers be included in Hall of Fame voting. Cooperstown took heed and formed a special committee to address the issue, initially planning to honor Negro Leaguers in a *separate* wing of the museum. This callous idea was soon scrapped. But not before Satchel Paige, the Negro League committee's first inductee in 1971, got wind of it. Upon learning that he would be honored in the "special" wing reserved for black players, he said, referring to himself in the third person, "The only change is that baseball has turned Paige from a second-class citizen to a second-class immortal."

My middle brother had polio in the 1950s. Because of his handicap, people were always doing very nice things for him. Ted Williams gave him an autographed baseball. We were so naive in those days. It was a nice thing, but not something we realized the monetary value of. That baseball was used in so many sandlot games in the neighborhood. . . . Last I saw of it, the signature was indecipherable. SIGH!

—Pat, 65

SECTION TWO

The Foul Pole Is Fair

*A*s you now know, Alexander Joy Cartwright is considered one of baseball's early founders. In the mid-1800s, the game's rules were designed to make it more challenging than its predecessors, cricket and rounders. (Shhhh.) Fortunately for all of us, he didn't get too fancy. And even after a slew of changes over the years, baseball remains fairly uncomplicated. At its most basic, baseball is about hitting, running, catching, and throwing; at its most complicated, it's about how not to spill your beverage while tracking the game's action on a stadium-issued scorecard with infuriatingly miniscule boxes. OK, someone can probably come up with something a little more challenging, but on some days, keeping those two things straight is downright maddening.

It's easy to remember some baseball rules because many of the basics are based on the number three. And, if you think about it, lots of great things come in threes. Consider the Three Musketeers. The Three Tenors. And who among us can forget the day we learned Newton's three laws of motion? Certain quotes even come to mind: "Veni, vidi, vici" and, "Yada, yada, yada."

So, it looks like baseball is in some pretty good company, doesn't it? And if you remember that it is a game of threes, the battle is half won. There are three strikes, three bases, and three outs given to each team per inning. If you want to stretch this concept, remember that fans plan for at least nine innings in each game, which, for all you math wizards out there, is a multiple of three. But why, you may ask, is beer only sold through the seventh inning? Seven is not a multiple of three. But we digress . . .

CHAPTER 9

Some of the Parts

Throughout the season, teams play games against each other in groups called "series." A series can be as few as two games and as many as four games. When one team wins them all, it's called a "sweep." When two teams split the first two games in a three-game series, the final game is called the "rubber match." Why do they call it a rubber match? Go ahead, hazard a guess. It would be just as good as our guess.

Half of a team's 162-game season is spent on the road. Depending on what team they play for, players can log thousands upon thousands of miles in a plane and often spend months away from their families.

Once the teams get settled into their hotel rooms, they'll head to the park to play the first game in a series. They start by warming up and having batting practice, or "BP," as it's sometimes referred to. Now, they're ready to play ball! If you are sitting in the seats close to homeplate, you might hear the umpire say just those words over the din of the crowd.

As mentioned previously, a baseball game is played out over a series of nine innings. One inning is made up of two halves—the top half, during which the visiting team tries to score runs and the bottom half, when the home team is at bat. The reference to top and bottom comes from how

the game looks on the stadium scoreboard or box score, which is a printed game summary. Stats for the visiting team are on the top because they get first crack at scoring, and stats for the home team are recorded on the bottom row. Each half inning gives the team the chance to score as many times as possible before racking up three outs.

A player can get an out in a variety of ways. One way for a batter to get out is when a player from the other team catches his batted ball before it lands. This is why fans see so many fielders running and diving for balls—they are trying to get to them before they hit the ground. Another way to get out is when a fielder tags a runner with the hand or glove that is holding the ball. This is called "making the tag." This is another reason why you'll see a runner diving or sliding into a base; he's hoping to avoid the tag. Occasionally you'll see a player get caught up in a "hot box," which is a rare but somewhat comical occurrence that happens when a runner gets stuck between bases and the defense dashes around like the Keystone Cops trying to get him out by tagging him with the ball.

The different ways a player can get out are numerous. It's sometimes a wonder that teams ever get around to scoring at all before collecting three outs. And some games are like that. Sometimes neither team scores until far into the game, or very few runs are scored during the whole game. When this happens, it's typically called a "pitcher's duel," because pitchers are given a lot of credit when the other team fails to score. You'll read more about their influence over the outcome of games in Section Five, *"A Schoolboy's Perfect Profession,"* but, just to let you know, when the offenses of both teams are somewhat shut down—resulting in a low-scoring game—both pitchers are said to have pitched good games. *En garde*!

On April 15, 1968, the Mets' Tom Seaver was fresh off his Rookie of the Year season when he pitched the first part of an excruciating pitcher's duel against the Houston Astros that went scoreless for twenty-three innings—more than six hours. Though that was quite the skirmish, the two teams showed less spunk for much of the remaining season, battling each other for last place in the National League. Twenty seasons later, Orel Hershiser participated in a few pitcher's duels on the way to helping his Dodgers win the 1988 World Series. Starting late August that year, he pitched fifty-nine scoreless innings, an MLB record.

Now that you know how the innings work, you'll be better able to decipher a few things. For example, when you hear that Hadlee got a hit in the

top of the eighth inning, you'll know that he plays for the visiting team. Bradman's hit in the bottom of the third? He's a home boy. And, yes, we were just about to mention Bill Mazeroski, the second baseman for the Pittsburgh Pirates. His dramatic, bottom-of-the-ninth home run won Pittsburgh the 1960 World Series title over the Yankees. Imagine sitting in that stadium. You know that everyone around you is going crazy, right?

Let's not be duped into thinking that there are always nine innings in a game. Sometimes there are more, and sometimes there are less. Games are occasionally called early by the umpires because of too much rain, for example. Players and fans will tolerate some rain, but after a while the game can get messy and downright dangerous. Among other considerations, such as lightning, the peril that comes from a slick, 90-mph fastball slipping out of the pitcher's hand and beaning a batter in the head carries great weight when umpires decide whether to cancel or postpone a game. What about an earthquake? Certainly, no one would expect to continue the game under those extreme circumstances, right? Well, since we had time to look this stuff up, we'll spare you the suspense. An earthquake struck the San Francisco Bay area on May 13, 2002, during the ninth inning of a game between the San Francisco Giants and the Atlanta Braves. The quake rocked the bleachers and rattled the glass in the press boxes, but the game never even paused. During a break in play, Jerry Lee Lewis' "Whole Lotta Shakin' Goin' On" played for the tenacious crowd. But we also know that earthquakes aren't always so benign. The catastrophic Loma Prieta earthquake thrashed the same area in 1989. It hit just before Game Three of the 1989 World Series between cross-Bay rivals, the San Francisco Giants and the Oakland A's. Since cameras were rolling to prepare for the game, viewers across the country witnessed some of the devastation as televisions caught concrete falling from Candlestick Park while the teams warmed up. As a result of the earthquake, the series was suspended ten days; in the end, Oakland swept the Giants.

Natural disasters aside, the most common reason why a game won't go a full nine innings is a compassionate gesture to the losing guests. If the visiting team is behind after the top of the ninth inning, the home team doesn't bother batting in the bottom half of the last inning because there would be no reason for the team to try to score more runs—they've already won! When the home team is winning after the top of the ninth, the game lasts only eight and a half innings and everyone goes home a little ear-

lier. Actually, there are really only two reasons a game does go a full nine innings: when the game is tied or the home team is losing after the top of the ninth. When either of these is true, the home team goes to bat in the bottom of the ninth in an attempt to win the game.

When a full nine innings of play results in a tied score, the game goes into "extra innings," starting with the top of the tenth. Whether the visitors score a run or not, the home team comes up in the bottom of the tenth to try to even the score or win the game. This is called "fair ups," and it's designed so that each team gets an equal chance of scoring. If the game is still tied at the end of the tenth inning the game will go into an eleventh inning, and so on, and so on.

A May 1984 marathon game between the Chicago White Sox and the Milwaukee Brewers took two days to finish. With the game tied 3-3 after seventeen innings, the game was suspended at 1:05 A.M. on the first day. The game resumed the next day and continued for another excruciating eight innings. Finally, after a total eight hours and six minutes, the White Sox triumphed, 7-6, on a Harold Baines home run in the bottom of the twenty-fifth inning. This is the longest game, time-wise, that has ever been played in the majors. The two teams dusted off the excitement of the contest and immediately faced off in their scheduled third game of the series, which ended in two hours and nine minutes. Chicago won the rubber match, 5-4.

Many fans regard these extra-inning games as representative of the true nature and excitement of the game. While it's true that there are many epic extra-inning games, it's equally true that there are many memorable games that end within nine innings. And not everyone welcomes the drama that comes with a game that ambles past midnight on a Tuesday, as it did in Chicago in 1984. We know a great many fans who have to go to work in the morning or are paying a babysitter $10 an hour and can't afford, for one reason or another, to hang around to see the conclusion. And, remember, beer sales ended hours ago. If you cannot or do not want to stay, you will surely have to shake off the belligerent stares—and perhaps comments—from fans who cannot fathom leaving such a sensational game. However, we believe that somewhere, sometime, a self-proclaimed "real" fan has received a call from the babysitter in the bottom of the twelfth inning to say that Little Suzy is barfing on the living room couch. Sometimes even baseball snobs have to leave games early.

Despite efforts to keep games from ending in a tie, they sometimes do. Before air travel was common, teams would agree upon a time to end the last game of a series so that visiting teams would be able to catch the train out of town. And, since lights were not introduced to ballparks until 1935, darkness served as a game clock of sorts for many games in the first half of the twentieth century. Game Two of the 1922 World Series between the New York Giants and the New York Yankees ended in a 3-3 tie when the game was called due to darkness after ten innings. Much like the display after the shortened 2002 All-Star Game, fans were incensed. They littered the field with paraphernalia, such as seat cushions and bottles, and argued that there was plenty of daylight left to keep playing. The Giants won the series, four games to none, and, to placate the fans, the league commissioner donated the $120,000 ticket sales of the tied game to charity.

Baseball has always been [a] part of my life. I grew up with nine kids, so we had our own team and played every day during the summer. Today it still brings us together, always going to ball games. It's a great game, and I've always enjoyed playing and watching with friends and family.

—Judy, 39

CHAPTER 10

Hitting the Basics

*K*nowing that the pitcher stands on the pitcher's mound and pitches the ball to the batter, who stands in the batter's box and waits for a good pitch to hit is a baseball fundamental. From the pitcher's perspective, a good pitch is something that the batter cannot hit well, if at all. However, from the batter's perspective, a good pitch is something that he thinks he can meet with a quality swing of the bat. Depending on the hitter, maybe that swing would produce a titanic home run. For many, however, a good swing that results in a hard-hit ball gives the batter a legitimate chance to run to first base—or beyond. And if he actually makes it to one of the bases, he has earned a "base hit," one of seven ways a batter can get on base.

The best professional players connect for a hit only once every three chances. What if you showed up for work late two-thirds of the time? You wouldn't have a job for long. If you showed up to play baseball and hit the ball one-third of the time, you'd not only have a job, you'd get paid a good deal of money. In fact, that kind of hitting equates to a .333 batting average (pronounced "three thirty-three"). If you ended the season hitting .333, you would likely be in contention for winning that season's batting title, which goes to the player with the highest batting average in each league.

Batting average is one of the most-recited—and perhaps overemphasized—benchmarks measuring a player's offensive skill. The number generally shows how often a player hits the ball. It is calculated by taking a player's number of hits and dividing it by the number of "at bats" he has had. Though there are some considerations that go into what an official at bat is, it can generally be thought of as how many chances a player gets to hit the ball. A good player is likely to have about four at bats during a typical nine-inning game. So, if said player gets two hits in his four at bats during a game, his day's batting average would be .500. A fine outing! A ball is considered a "hit" when the player gets on any base safely by his own doing—not by way of a mistake or choice made by the other team or any other fluke.

When games go into extra innings, players get more at bats. On June 23, 1993, the Seattle Mariners' Jay Buhner had seven at bats during the Mariners' fourteen-inning win over the Oakland A's. Those extra at bats during that close 8-7 game made it possible for him to "hit for the cycle," which is a rare feat when a player hits a single, double, triple, and a home run in one game. To make Buhner's accomplishment sweeter, his home run in the bottom of the first inning was not just an ordinary home run; it was a grand slam. For added flavor, his last at bat was the triple that set up the winning run, which so happened to be . . . him. Quite a day!

While there are several factors that can either inflate or undercut one's batting average, it is a figure that has withstood the test of time. Poor hitters who come close to batting only .200 ("two hundred") are said to flirt with the "Mendoza Line." Though the Line is widely known to be named after Mario Mendoza, it could have just as easily been in tribute to Minnie or Carlos Mendoza. The three weren't brothers, but they shared a last name and an eerie inability to hit the baseball very often. At the other end of the spectrum, Hall of Famer Ted Williams hit .406 ("four-oh-six") while playing for Boston in 1941. This is just before he took a four-year break from the game to serve in World War II. Breaking the .400 mark is an accomplishment that, like Williams himself, stands frozen in time.

A player like Williams is helpful to his team because his high average shows an ability to get on base often. And if a player can get on base, he can score runs. The more often he's on base, the more often he'll score. It's that simple. Lots of guys with high batting averages also score the most runs. Williams topped the league in batting average seven times and runs

scored six times during his career. Conversely, a career's worth of runs from all three Mendozas still didn't surpass the number of runs Ted Williams scored in a typical season.

But there are many players who don't have the finesse with the bat as Williams did. Unlike the Mendoza contingent, who couldn't hit much at all, others table the high batting average yet carve out a place at the plate as power hitters. It's not a bad trade-off; a player who hits for power is someone who gets lots of extra-base hits, or reaches any base other than first, which is a single. These types of power players can be best gauged by looking at their slugging percentage. Similar to batting average, which divides hits by at bats, slugging percentage divides *total bases* by at bats. Total bases is how many bases a player touches. So, if a player hits a single, he touches one base. When he hits a triple, he touches three. A home run? He has touched four bases, though touching home is not really a base, per se, because it's called home *plate*. Semantics aside, a home run counts as four bases. When you add up all the bases a player has touched during the course of a game, a season, or a career, you'll have figured out his total bases. Divide that number by his at bats and you've got his slugging percentage. The disparity between a player's batting average and his slugging percentage indicates whether a player is much of a slugger or not. Because slugging calculation gives extra credit to those powerful extra-base hits, it's easy to see why there was so much hoopla around a player like Mark "Big Mac" McGwire and his modest career batting average. The reason that we're still talking about him—aside from his suspect role in the league's steroid abuses of the late 1990s—is because of his 583 career homers and his ensuing .588 lifetime slugging percentage, which is 300 points higher than his batting average.

Baseball watchers say that McGwire, and those like him, don't hit for average but, rather, they hit for power. As far as McGwire is concerned, this is true. While McGwire's sixteen-year, .263 batting average was respectable, especially for a power hitter, he never came close to winning a batting title. Why don't these guys hit for high average? It's because players like McGwire often have one-dimensional swings. They swing big and fail to make contact with a lot of pitches. This is a fancy way of saying they strike out a lot, which can bring down their batting averages.

Then there are those guys who have it all, like Babe Ruth, who hit for average *and* power. He tops the career list with a slugging percentage of

.690, while his career batting average was .342—tenth on the all-time list. Similarly, Ted Williams is number two on the all-time sluggers list and seventh on the batting-average list.

It is rare and amazing when a player finishes the season leading his league in batting average, home runs, *and* runs batted in (RBI, or "ribbie"). When this happens, or if he's tied for the top spot in any of those categories, the player has stumbled upon one of baseball's trifectas, the "Triple Crown" of hitting. The achievement shows not only a player's talent to hit for big power and high average, but also how many runs a player contributes. The latter factor is somewhat quantifiable by counting up a player's RBI, which is given whenever a batter gets a hit that scores a run for his team. For example, if there are two runners on base and the batter hits a home run, three runs score—the two baserunners and the batter. Thus, the batter gets three RBI for that one hit.

The Triple Crown has been awarded only fourteen times. Babe Ruth never won it, though he came close. He led the league in both homers and RBI in six seasons during his career but none of these years coincided with 1924, the one year he won the batting title. Ted Williams and Rogers Hornsby, a Hall of Famer who retired in 1937, are the only two players to snag the Triple Crown twice. And Williams narrowly missed two other times. He would have nabbed another in 1941, the year he hit .406, if it weren't for DiMaggio and those pesky five extra RBI. And on the last day of the 1949 season, Hall of Famer George Kell scarcely beat Williams out for batting average, .3429 to .3427. This was Kell's only batting title.

Glory came back to Boston twenty years after Williams won his second Triple Crown for the Red Sox in 1947. In fact, the fall of 1967 was an exciting time for the area. After future Hall of Famer Carl Yastrzemski led his team through a stressful pennant race, the team went to the World Series for the first time since Williams' Boston team lost to the St. Louis Cardinals in the 1946 Fall Classic. As if that wasn't enough for one city to handle, Deidre was born in a nearby hospital during Game Six, and Yastrzemski capped off a fine season by winning the Triple Crown. He was the last player to do so. That year he batted .326, had 121 RBI, and hit forty-four home runs, which Minnesota's Harmon Killebrew tied in the penultimate game of the season against Boston. After all of that excitement, we imagine Yastrzemski was looking forward to hoisting his Triple Crown trophy. Winners do get trophies, right? Right. So you might wonder

why Yaz doesn't have a trophy. Perhaps you thought the slight was because of the troublesome tie with Killebrew. That would be a good guess. Or maybe you didn't even realize that he doesn't have a trophy. Well, the story is that Yastrzemski did get one but returned it when he noticed that his last name was misspelled. While it was being corrected, or so he thought, he was sent a fruit bowl from the American League to tide him over. We're pretty sure it was intended for the ballplayer. The card was addressed to "Charles." Hope he managed to enjoy the fruit because he never got a corrected trophy.

Someone who has a lot of RBI can epitomize a team player or show that he is a "clutch" performer. Such a player always seems to be able to get the big hit when the team most needs one. It's debatable if someone can truly be depended upon in such situations. But there are those who still argue it. For what it's worth, it is often said that the New York Yankee Derek Jeter is a clutch player. For you Red Sox fans, there's some talk that David Ortiz is "King of Clutch." To your corners!

But it cannot be overlooked that a player with high RBI speaks volumes about the guy's teammates. After all, the other blokes are on base often enough that they can be batted in to score with some frequency. They must be pretty good themselves. Take Jeter's teammate, Alex Rodriguez, who is considered the anti-clutch hitter, yet still led the league with 156 RBI in 2007. Rodriguez's reputation for choking in big games was well-earned; every time he had a chance to redeem himself, he'd blow it. In fact, by 2008, his postseason batting slump dated back to the 2004 AL Championship Series against Boston when he went 8-31, with two dastardly days where he didn't get a hit at all. But his 2007 RBI statistic has little to do with whether his clutch is broken or not. Rather, it has a lot to do with the fact that Rodriguez was batting fourth with Johnny Damon, Jeter, and Bobby Abreu—all high on-base percentage guys—hitting before him. It also had something to do with his league-leading fifty-four home runs. That's more than a third of his RBI, right there! Hmmm. RBI and homers? Sounds like the makings of a Triple Crown, doesn't it? You'd be correct in thinking that but, for Rodriguez, the Triple Crown eluded him in 2007 because his .314 batting average landed him in thirteenth place for his league's batting title. But he nabbed the league's MVP. Who needs clutch? Or a fruit basket, for that matter.

I just remember my mom getting excited about watching Ted Williams and yelling, "Go Teddy Boy." We knew she was really enjoying herself! He was also a spokesperson for the Jimmy Fund in Boston and encouraged children to raise funds—which I did by having a "show" for neighbor kids in the backyard with a blanket over the clothesline as the stage. We raised over $3.00 for the Jimmy Fund that helped sick kids and felt pretty proud of ourselves!

—Donna, 62

## CHAPTER 11

It Takes More Than Balls

There are many ways for a player to react to a pitch, some spectacular, and a few unspectacular. Some will get a player on base, while others will result in an out for the team, like when the batter hits a long fly ball to the outfielder who, somewhat predictably, makes the catch, or the blooper hit up the middle of the infield that is swept up by the shortstop who, also predictably, makes the throw to first base for the out. In both cases the batter literally hit the ball but didn't get credit for a "hit." This is the baseball world, remember. Much is not as it seems.

A single pitch can end up with a number of different outcomes. Sometimes it gets hit, but most of the time, a pitch results in either a ball, strike, or foul. Fans can keep track of how the hitter fares at each plate appearance by knowing the "count." The count tells the fan how the duel between hitter and pitcher is panning out. A count may look something like 2-1 ("two and one"). This means that the batter has two balls and one strike. Balls are always the first number in the count and strikes are recorded

second. As for foul balls, a player can hit an unlimited amount of these. (You'll also read in Chapter 13, "Something Has Run Afoul," that foul balls are compelling entertainment.)

Having said that, let's start with the first number in the count, which is called a "ball." You already know that pitchers pitch and hitters hit. Or, at least they try to. Well, meet the umpire. He umps. Yes, that's a verb. One of his responsibilities is calling the "strike zone." The strike zone is an ethereal space between the batter's knees and chest, directly above home plate. The ump determines whether the pitcher delivered even a portion of the ball in the strike zone. The pitcher isn't required to do this, but it's worth his time if he does so. The batter chooses whether or not to swing at any given pitch. He can swing at pitches inside or outside the strike zone. If he chooses not to swing at a ball that is outside the zone, it's ruled a ball. Pitchers are allowed to throw three such pitches—those out of the strike zone that the batter doesn't swing at. If the pitcher opens with three straight balls, the count would be 3-0 ("three and oh"). If a fourth "ball" is thrown, the batter is given a free pass, or a "walk," to first base. If the pitcher does this throughout the game, he's having a hard time "finding the strike zone." If he does it throughout the season, he'll be finding the bus station.

Using those criteria, Philadelphia's Mitch Williams, a.k.a "Wild Thing," might have had a Greyhound ticket in his back pocket, just in case. Not only is he famous for giving up a World Series-ending home run to Toronto's Joe Carter in 1993, he's also the only pitcher in history with significant playing time who gave up more walks than hits. In fact, he walked about seven batters per nine innings pitched. Still, he made a living as a respected pitcher for the better part of eleven years—more power to him. Then there is Bruno Haas, who was born on May 5, 1891, which just so happens to be the same day that well-heeled New York society types paid upwards of two dollars to see Peter Ilyich Tchaikovsky conduct the opening concert at New York's Carnegie Hall. That was certainly more than people would pay to see Haas pitch. On June 23, 1915, he had an unfortunate major league debut. Pitching for the Philadelphia A's in the second game of a double-header, Haas walked sixteen Yankees on the way to a 15-7 loss. By season's end, he was demoted to the minor leagues.

Occasionally, and for various reasons, pitchers intentionally walk batters. They do this by purposefully pitching the ball outside the strike zone. This still takes four pitches. It's interesting because, before each throw, the pitcher

seems to pretend to plan to throw a real pitch. And the batter squares up, pretending to prepare to take a real pitch. But there are no secrets here. They both know the intentional walk is in the make. Intentional or not, a walk is the second way a batter can get on base. When this happens it is said that the hitter got a base on balls (BB).

If a pitcher hits the batter with a pitch, the batter usually gets a free trip to first base. But not all the time. If you are inclined, this might be the time to start thumbing through some of baseball's more arcane rules. Hit by pitch (HBP) is the third of seven ways a batter to can get on base.

When I was in elementary school, I knew baseball from TV (Mickey Mantle, Sandy Koufax, Whitey Ford), but didn't really get interested until fourth grade. I was into reading biographies of famous historical figures back then. That year, I won our school's geography bee and the prize was three books from our little paperback book store. The only biography they had was that of Ty Cobb. In addition to getting me permanently hooked on baseball, it was the first time I had seen the words "goddamn" and "son-of-a-bitch" in print.

—Beth, 48

## CHAPTER 12

Strike the Ball Next Time

$\mathcal{B}$efore it was a political statement, the "Three strikes and you're out" rule was part of baseball's lexicon. The rule was created to keep the game moving so batters wouldn't stand around waiting for a perfect pitch to smack. Some fans complain that today's game is too slow. Imagine how dawdling it would be without the umpire enforcing the strike zone, wielding the power to call balls and strikes.

There are some tricky ways a batter can get saddled with a strike. The two typical strikes are a "swing and a miss" and a "called strike." A swing and a miss is, somewhat obviously, what happens when the batter swings the bat and misses the ball. As we mentioned earlier, power-hitting numbers seem to go hand-in-hand with swinging big and missing bigger. And it isn't more evident than with Hall of Famer Reggie Jackson, who was the slugger to be slugged with during the 1970s. Early in Jackson's career, batting great Joe DiMaggio tried to craft Jackson's swing in order to reduce

his strikeouts. It didn't work. Jackson retired after twenty-one seasons with 2,597 strikeouts, an MLB record.

Not all strikes are of the "swing and miss" variety. There are the times when the umpire thinks the batter should have been able to hit the pitch—it was in the strike zone, you know—but the batter never swung as the ball went past him. Perhaps the batter thought it was out of the strike zone. Unfortunately, it's not up to him. Nor is it up to the group of fans yelling, "No way! That was low and outside!" It doesn't matter what anyone else thinks. It only matters what the ump thought. If the batter doesn't swing and the ump thinks it was in the strike zone, the batter is tagged with a strike. A batter may react emotionally when an ump calls a strike, but since an umpire can eject a player from the game for "arguing balls and strikes," the batter must mask his frustration carefully. The batter's irritation often peaks when the third strike is called by the umpire—resulting in an out for the team. When this happens, it's said that the batter was called out on strikes or "struck out looking" because he just watched his last strike go by. It is also referred to as a "punch out," based on the flourish that some umpires put into the call, seemingly to amplify the embarrassment shouldered by the batter.

During a July 2004 game against the Los Angeles Dodgers, David Ortiz of the Boston Red Sox struck out looking and was tossed from the game for, to hear him tell it, "just asking questions" of the umpire. He went back to his dugout where he proceeded to throw his bats onto the field, narrowly missing the Dodgers' first base coach. The whole outburst earned him a five-game suspension from playing. Afterward, during an apology, he said, "I didn't mean to hit anybody, I just wanted to throw my bats out there. . . ." And the ump just wanted to throw you out. Even Steven.

If you are keeping close track of the batter's at bat, or plate appearance—or if you're just tuning back into the game—remember that strikes are the second number in the count. You may hear something like "Polansky has a 1-2 count" ("one and two" count). That means he has one ball and two strikes against him. One more strike and Polansky will be heading back to the dugout in shame.

In the next section we'll talk about other ways to get strikes. Can't wait? We can't either, so here's a little something to whet your appetite for the topic: bunts and foul balls are to other ways a batter can earn a strike.

I like the history that baseball has. To think that this game was played before the 1900s, lasted through two World Wars, and brought us so many historical figures . . . What other sport can claim the history that baseball can? Whatever horrible thing there was that happened in history, there was always baseball there to help us through it.

—Ramona, 42

Something Has Run Afoul

One of the game's early rules was intended to create a defined playing field and to require the batter to keep the ball "fair" or "in bounds" according to the lines on the field. These changes forced the batter to hit with a level of control that wasn't required in, say, the games of rounders and cricket. (Not that these games had anything to do with baseball.) The two foul lines on a baseball field start at home plate and go, respectively, through first and third bases. They continue all the way to the outfield walls in right and left fields and into oblivion. Any ball that lands between those lines is considered fair and playable. If the ball bounces and rolls out before ever traveling as far as first or third base, the hit is counted as foul.

When a ball is hit out of bounds, the batter doesn't have to run to first base. A ball that is hit foul gives the batter another chance to get a hit. In fact, as long as batters keep hitting balls that land or roll foul—sometimes into a fan's glove, lap, or popcorn—they get an unlimited number of chances to get a hit and run to first base.

That is a basic knowledge of foul territory. There are some obscure rules regarding when a ball is called foul, such as the instances mentioned above about where the ball bounces or how far it travels. But if you are ever wondering if a ball has gone foul, look at the umpires. If they are pointing toward the field, the ball was fair. If they raise both hands in the air, the ball was foul. If they start doing the hokey-pokey, then you know it's time to go.

Depending on where you are sitting, foul balls are your best chance at leaving a game with an official MLB baseball. My, it is unthinkable how many times we have seen fans dash across and over seats, children, and the elderly to chase down a foul ball. A foul can be a screaming line-drive into the fans sitting on the third base side of the stadium, or a long fly ball to the upper deck of seats. Perhaps it's a slow roller that inches its way along the baseline before it finally, agonizingly, crosses the line and becomes foul. Sometimes it's a bunt that rolls foul or a pop-up behind the catcher.

It's not unusual for a batter to "foul off" a few balls, but some batters have the ability to make contact with any type of pitch. Often a good contact hitter is one of the best hitters on his team or in the league. Some are known to "chase" pitches that are well outside the strike zone. Why doesn't the hitter just allow these pitches to go by and be called balls? Maybe it's pride. Contact hitters do what they do best, and letting hittable pitches go past may not be their nature. And they probably like to frustrate pitchers. While a typical batter may allow a ball to go by or wait for a "good" pitch that he can hit into play, these unusually patient contact hitters can foul off even bad pitches in order to stay alive at the plate and get a chance to see another pitch. Maybe that next one will be the perfect one. Patient hitters test pitchers' patience because it takes hurlers lots of extra pitches to get guys like this out. And it can also become mentally exasperating. When a batter does this he is said to be "working the count."

One such batter was Philadelphia Hall of Famer Richie Ashburn, who played in the mid-1900s. His Hall of Fame plaque says that Ashburn had a "superb knowledge of the strike zone," but it doesn't mention how his talent took a maniacal turn. Ashburn was curiously capable at fouling off balls. The real madness came in August of 1957 when, as usual, Ashburn was fouling off pitches into the stands. One hit the wife of a local sports writer and broke her nose. The game was suspended for a few minutes as medics tended to her. When the game resumed, Ashburn fouled off the

 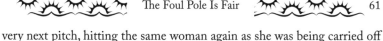

very next pitch, hitting the same woman again as she was being carried off on a stretcher.

Other stories have Chicago White Sox shortstop Luke "Luscious" Appling fouling off pitches in the 1930s to get back at his team's owner, Charlie Comiskey, the ballsy, tight-fisted fellow that we've already mentioned a few times. Appling surmised that the more balls he fouled off into the stands, the more balls the owner would have to buy. Then, there's the cantankerous Detroit Tiger Ty Cobb who is said to have routinely—and purposefully—sent foul balls into the opposing team's dugout for the delight of seeing his adversaries scatter for life and limb. And that was when he was feeling nice.

Stadium layout often determines whether a foul ball will be caught for an out or will provide another chance for the batter to swing the bat and possibly get a hit. Some ballparks sport a big, grassy, and level foul area. This is the area between the foul line and the stadium seats. If a batter hits a ball in that area, a fielder may effortlessly run into foul territory and catch the ball for an out. Other stadiums have a small foul area where the seats are built to hug the foul line, making the same hit land in the tenth row of fans. This results in a souvenir for the fan—not an out. In stadiums with small foul territory, hitters are more likely to foul off a lot of balls simply because fielders can't clamber up and over rows of fans to catch the ball for the out, nor are they allowed to. If a hitter keeps fouling balls into the stands, he gets to swing at more pitches. Perhaps the next one will land him safely on first base. Because hitters profit from such a layout, a stadium's foul territory is one measure of what makes it a "hitter's park" or not. Take a look at the foul territory the next time you go to a little league game. Or take note of your major league team's stadium and compare it to other MLB parks. Then take this information and add into the equation how far a player needs to hit a ball to clear the outfield fences for a home run. Pretty soon you can start drawing some conclusions about why certain players do better in certain stadiums.

Putting the foul ball in context with strikes and the count, in general, takes a bit of attention to the game. Though batters can hit foul balls indefinitely, they are reined in by the fact that, if there are less than two strikes in the count, hits that are called as foul balls are considered strikes. But once the batter has two strikes he can continue hitting foul balls into the stands for eternity because the final strike cannot be a "hit" foul ball. On the other

hand, balls that are bunted—not hit—are always considered strikes. The only time a foul ball will be the last strike, then, is when the batter intended to bunt. Wait! Please don't leave.

So, to recap, if Sobers comes up to bat and swings and misses, or "whiffs," the first pitch, his count will be 0-1 ("oh and one;" which means no balls, one strike). If he hits a foul ball into the stands on the next pitch, the count will go to 0-2. Since there were fewer than two strikes in the count, the foul ball was counted as a strike. Now, he's sitting on his final strike. Sobers can keep fouling off the pitches because foul balls cannot be the third strike. However, he may swing with less abandon since he's facing an 0-2. A cavalier swing may result in the third strike, which will land him back in the dugout.

And consider this at bat: Pollock comes up to bat, and the pitcher throws two back-to-back bona fide strikes; the count goes to a precarious 0-2. Then, when Pollock hits the next pitch foul, the count will still be 0-2, because a hit foul ball cannot count as the final strike. Had he bunted the ball and it rolled foul, it would have counted as the final strike. Before a 1903 rule change, foul balls were never ruled as strikes. This means that, at the turn of the twentieth century, baseball generally experienced longer at bats with more foul balls sprayed over the grandstand.

The guardians of long-ball foul territory are the foul poles towering over left and right fields that help umpires determine whether a high fly ball is fair or foul. If a ball sails by on the field side of the pole, it's fair and a home run. If the ball flies by on the other side of the pole, it's foul. Some may choose to refer to these poles as the "fair poles" in order to remember the rule that, if a long-fly ball hits the foul pole, that the ball is fair and considered a home run, regardless of where the ball may land.

Note to self: No one really refers to them out loud as the "fair" poles.

However, before 1931, when a long ball passed the foul pole on the fair side, it wasn't ruled a home run if the ball curved and then *landed* on the other side of the imaginary foul line that extends into oblivion. The ball could leave the stadium a home run and there was much rejoicing. But when an umpire saw that that the home run ball actually landed in foul territory—maybe somewhere in a mud flat—it was then considered a foul ball. The home run was negated, and the batter got to see another pitch. Not that he wanted to. He wanted that home run back. Babe Ruth's prime years were affected by this rule and, according to baseball historian

Bill Jenkinson, dozens of his home runs were reversed during that time period because of it. Jenkinson concludes that, because of this pre-1931 rule, instead of the 714 homers he hit, the Babe would have had about 765 career homers by today's standards. This is a few more home runs than Barry Bonds and Hammerin' Hank Aaron, whose 755 career home runs was the major league record until 2007. It was in that year that Bonds, under a shroud of steroid-related controversy, finished the season with 762 homers.

I have lots of great baseball memories. My son was six months old and was beaned in the diaper by a foul ball. He barely took the time away from nursing to make a short whimper and then back to feeding.

—Debbie, 50

Chapter 14

Run Like You Mean It

There are many things that point to what is valued in baseball. Just look at the existing stats: there are loads of hitting stats, but only a few for running. No one hears about someone being a shoe-in for the Hall of Fame because he led the league in stolen bases eight seasons in a row, or ran 100 meters in less than nine seconds. No—it's all about the hitting. This isn't surprising, but every now and again, it's worth mentioning.

The running game is so maligned that sometimes players don't even run when they are supposed to. We're not talking about the guys who run like they are carrying a piano on their backs. We're talking about the guys who are just lazy. It's as if all they want to do is hit. Well, we're here to tell you that when the batter hits the ball, he is expected to run hard to first base in an effort to get there before someone throws the ball and gets him out. Sure, some players naturally run faster than others, but they are all expected to try hard to get to first base safely.

Why is it, then, that fans see runners, after hitting a ball, not trying very hard to get to first base? Are they bored with the whole thing? It's hard to speculate, really. If we had the chance, believe us, we'd run hard! Not fast, mind you, because that would be impossible. But we'd break a sweat. And that would probably happen about halfway to first base. Anyway, often a ball player's lack of hustle has something to do with frustration. Specifically, if he didn't hit the ball very well, he figures that he'll probably be thrown out at first, anyway. So, why bother running hard? His mother would tell him to stop sulking. So would we.

In an egregious display of pouting during a September 2002 game, Boston's Manny Ramirez hit a grounder to the Tampa Bay pitcher and, instead of hightailing it to first base, he immediately turned to walk back to the dugout. Sure, he likely would have been thrown out long before reaching first base. But, had he run, maybe the pitcher would have made a bad throw to first base that would have allowed Ramirez to arrive at the bag safely. We will never know. When he hit a home run later in the game, he ran the bases. The homer clearly pleased him. However, his embarrassing and lackluster play in the beginning of the game wasn't overlooked by team management; he was fined an undisclosed amount for lack of effort. That's a fancy way of saying that he was behaving like a Sissy Mary.

The attitude of players like Ramirez is in stark contrast to Cincinnati Reds non-Hall of Fame superstar Pete Rose, who was revered by the city's working-class fans. He played with so much effort that he was mockingly nicknamed "Charlie Hustle" in his early years as a ballplayer. Among other things, he patented the head-first dive and would routinely sprint to first base when he got a base on balls. You read that right, he ran when he got a walk. Maybe that's a little overkill: And maybe that's why he was mocked as a rookie. And there's Rex Hudler, whose unspectacular thirteen-year career ended in 1998 after playing with six different teams. But it was his spunk and upbeat demeanor that earned him fans wherever he went, as well as the nickname "Wonder Dog." Hudler said that he ran hard for the "guy in the stands who never played. That one-hopper back to the mound, I ran it out because that guy would have run it out, and I didn't want to cheat him."

One of the few statistics that reflects a player's speed is his number of stolen bases (SB). A stolen base is a bold offensive move that occurs when a baserunner advances to the next base in the short time it takes for the pitcher to pitch the ball to the batter. For this reason, a successful steal

requires an adroit runner with quickness and good instincts. Think: Ty Cobb, Lou Brock, or Rickey Henderson, who retired after the 2003 season with the record for most career base steals.

Clues to baseball's best runners are couched in their hitting numbers. For instance, someone who gets a lot of singles, or base hits, may simply get to first base often because he is a fast runner and has the speed to beat a throw from the field, earning base hits that slower players cannot. And sometimes the best runners aren't always the fastest; scrappy runners fluster fielders by swapping grit for a lack of speed, and when fielders get flustered, they can make mistakes on routine plays, such as missing an easy throw for an out. Runners who could bring about such fever are Pete Rose or David Eckstein, who was the St. Louis Cardinals' energetic shortstop and MVP of the 2006 World Series, which the Cards won. Pepper Martin played for the Cardinals in the 1930s and was known for being both fast and scrappy. A sportswriter wrote that Pepper "ran as though the devil himself were at his heels and he would let no obstacle, human or otherwise, stand in his way." Martin was an outfielder for the "Gashouse Gang," a nickname that reflected his team's unkempt appearance and brutish manner. But civility be damned: his Cardinals won six Championships between 1926 and 1946.

If a player has lots of triples—getting to third base with a single hit— chances are he's a fast runner because it takes someone speedy to cover that much ground while the outfielders are trying to get the ball back to the infield to force the runner to stop. This would be someone like Stan Musial, who played for the Cardinals during the 1940s. The Hall of Famer's .559 slugging percentage aptly reflected his 177 career triples—not to mention his 475 homers. Slow runners, on the other hand, rarely get to third base without the help of a fielder making a mistake. Remember "Big Mac" McGwire? He hit only six triples during sixteen seasons. A faster runner probably could have turned many of his 252 doubles into triples. But McGwire's work at the plate outweighed his deficient baserunning. Specifically, his 583 homers helped drive in 1,414 runs throughout his career.

But not everyone who is a big hitter is as agonizing to watch round second base like McGwire. Some guys are good runners. These guys belong to an exclusive club called the 40-40 ("forty-forty"). The four players who belong to this group have hit forty home runs *and* stolen forty bases in *one* season. They are Jose Canseco, Barry Bonds, Alex Rodriguez, and Alfonso

Soriano, who trumped the other members by also hitting forty doubles. Guess he's starting his own club, the 40-40-40. More frequent, though still rare, is when someone joins the 30-30 club. Thirty-two players are members, and a few have done it several times in their careers. Bobby Bonds and his son, Barry, are the only two who renewed their memberships five times during their careers.

Fans today are accustomed to watching home-run balls disappear into the bleachers, or into a fountain, or into San Francisco Bay, depending on what stadium you're visiting. These homers, while dramatic, are not the only kind.

Although rare, fast runners have turned well-hit balls into home runs just by running really fast around the bases while the fielders try to figure out where to throw the ball for the out. This is called an "inside-the-park" home run. These types of homers are certainly not uncommon in neighborhood little-league games. And even in major-league games—before 1920. This was the time when outfields were larger than they are today and well-hit balls would roll for a long time, giving runners ample time to round the bases for a home run. In those days, a line of rope that fans were required to stand behind often served as the outfield "fence." Sam "Wahoo Sam" Crawford, born in Wahoo, Nevada, in 1880, holds the modern-day major league record of fifty-one inside-the-park home runs. This represents more than half of his homers throughout a career that spanned from 1899 to 1917. In 1901 alone, Crawford ran out twelve inside-the-park homers and led his league in total home runs with sixteen. The contemporary record for inside-the-park homers is held by the Kansas City Royals' Willie Wilson. His thirteen inside-the-park homers represent a third of his career total. He led the league in triples five times throughout his nineteen-year career, beginning in 1976. In comparison, only one of Hank Aaron's 755 dingers was an inside-the-park homer. Aaron was all power, all the time.

Did you just see what happened there? It always comes back to hitting. Even in a measly chapter about running, there was the pull to talk about how great a hitter Hank Aaron was. Have we become part of the problem? Even Jackie Robinson—Aaron's hero—saw something special when Aaron was a twenty-year-old rookie. At the time, Robinson told a reporter, "You're going to be watching him hit for a long time." And he was right. But, for what it's worth, Aaron, as evidenced by his membership in the 30-30 club, was also a very good baserunner; it's just that running's not what puts food on the table.

As with most things, baseball is in the family. I played softball as a grade-schooler. At [age] ten, I wanted to grow up to be a professional player. But not being much good, or very competitive, not to mention a woman, I watch it mostly, rather than play.

—Ellen, 41

SECTION THREE

Managing Hardball and Hardheads

*T*here was a time—a long time ago—that baseball managers got some respect. This period didn't last terribly long. Things seemed to get worse with changes in the game, increasing media exposure, and technology that rendered any passing fan an "expert." Sure, some skippers are successful and loved. But there is no manager out there who hasn't endured time as the proverbial punching bag of entire cities. These guys get earfuls from fans and newspaper columnists. They get it from their players and team owners. Sometimes they even get it twice a day. And that's if they are lucky.

But, things weren't so bad until team owners started heaping work on managers in the late 1880s. Back then, all these guys really wanted to do was play some ball and act as what we may recognize as a team captain— someone who cordially meets with the other team and lays out the day's rules. These decisions could be as mundane as figuring out whether the maple in left field would be considered out of bounds or as gruesome as determining whether the bone sticking out of Polansky's leg would prohibit him from taking second base.

Then people started paying attention. Owners became keenly aware of baseball's growth potential and assigned team captains work that encouraged profit. You know, work that had to do with numbers. There were the huge piles of equipment bags to track, new strategy decisions to make, and captains started scouring train schedules to facilitate games in other towns. These new responsibilities made the job exhausting, but what were these jocks to do? Take it and shut up; there just weren't a lot of jobs around for baseball guys.

The fact remained that someone had to figure all this stuff out. Juggling fielders, pitchers, drama, and egos is no cushy job. Who would be masochist enough to sign up for this? Well, about 700 guys have tolerated the abuse since the game's beginning. Some worked for peanuts. Some worked for years. A few found glory. But many more withered along the periphery, waiting for their moment in the sun.

CHAPTER 15

Let's Take a Walk

Off we go down memory lane, to a time in the mid-1800s when running a team wasn't terribly complicated. Things were so informal that, occasionally, players wouldn't show up for a game and the rest of the team was left to rustle up some local layabouts just so they would be able to play with a full nine-man team.

By the mid-1860s, most teams had an official team leader, whom they called the captain. This title befit the post-Civil War era when most young men were accustomed to referring to leaders as such. The captain managed his team, coached them when to run, stay, or slide, and took the lead when it was time to talk—or argue—with the umpire.

Most teams ran peacefully in this manner until the 1880s, when changes in the game necessitated a leadership adjustment. Rules, which had been in near-constant flux for the better part of thirty years, became standardized, and owners started throwing serious money at their sporting ventures. Before long, players, fans, and investors became vocal about whether the team was doing well or why it wasn't and how Polansky was a wimp for not taking second. On the field, gallantry was dead and mischief born. Stolen bases, bunt plays, smack talk. Team S-P-I-R-I-T!

Baseball became more businesslike and teams started looking for new ways to win games and secure fan loyalty. For this reason, owners started toying with rules, such as allowing substitutions during the game, even for the able-bodied. This particular rule was expected to garner more offense, strategy, and fan excitement, and was officially adopted in 1891. Predictably, the change was met with derision from those who considered themselves among the game's purists.

One effect of the substitution rule change was roster bloat. With replacements allowed, teams snatched up as many players as they could afford, and player recruitment became fiercely competitive. Teams found creative ways to support this change in focus financially. More games, more concessions. More advertising—someone clearly had boodle on the brain.

With additional players, the captain organized his batting order differently. Before 1891, the team leader had only nine players to work with and there was no choice whether a guy was going to be in that day's lineup or not; they all had to play, or they'd be replaced by a town ruffian. After the rule change, however, teams had the luxury of weighing things, such as which hitters would fare best against the other team's pitcher.

Ultimately, the rigors created by the new substitution rule pushed the role of the traditional team captain off the plank. On some teams, another player took over leadership in the new order, while the captain maintained a figurehead position. The new player-manager may have had more business savvy or just more time to take on the added responsibilities. Not only did he schedule opponents, recruit players, make travel arrangements, and market games, he managed team strategy and tracked those colossal equipment bags.

As the nature of the game became increasingly complex, even the on-field responsibilities became specialized. During the latter part of the 1800s, these player-managers molded the game into the one that we now recognize. They decided on things such as when to have a batter take a pitch in the shoulder, steal a base, or lay down a bunt. This also marked the beginning of the "armchair manager," a fan who specializes in second-guessing the manager and pontificating about it. Before this point, there were very few choices, strategy or otherwise, that required that level of nattering criticism.

You need to fast-forward only 100 years to witness the fruition of the seed planted by the armchair managers in those early years. Whether loud

or thoughtful, we are now treated to pre-game and post-game shows. In between, we are treated to color commentary during the game. And let's not ignore the pull of magazines, sports pages, blogs, and entire cable networks devoted to commentary, condemnation, and kudos.

One of baseball's early fathers started this cacophony. Though other writers occasionally covered baseball, Henry Chadwick was a daily reporter and among the first to travel with a team, the Washington Nationals in 1867. It wasn't easy being a team reporter; teams wanted only good things written about them, and some reporters were threatened in an attempt to keep their newspaper accounts acceptable to the players. Sometimes, mere threats didn't satisfy the players. One catcher decked a reporter for writing something of which the player did not approve. Before sports writers were, as they are now, safely perched above home plate they watched the game alongside the dugout. This made them easy targets for displeased players. Chadwick even thought that players occasionally tried to intimidate reporters by hitting foul balls their way, à la Ty Cobb.

Criticism was perhaps the last thing the 1879 Chicago White Stockings, which later became known as the Cubs, were worried about. After winning the National League in 1876, the league's first year, the team since had fallen short of a championship and headed into its third straight season under the management of a different player. They wanted to reclaim that winning feeling. That year, the team's twenty-seven-year-old star first baseman Adrian "Cap" Anson took a stab at the position and led the team to its first winning season in three years. One of the best players of his time, Anson acted as the team's player-manager until 1897. The following year he had a brief twenty-two-game stint managing the New York Giants. Anson retired from managing with a .578 winning percentage, which is among the best in the game's history. And he was multi-talented; after retiring from baseball, he worked as the Chicago City Clerk, tried his hand in politics, and appeared in vaudeville, something he had dabbled in while still playing baseball.

It is partially because of player-managers like Anson that you still see baseball managers wearing uniforms. Back in the early 1900s, they used to run the show from the sidelines, bat their turn in the lineup, and then head out to play in the field. Wearing the team uniform started as an obvious practicality and has continued as tradition. Now, while managers look like they want to be called in to play right field, they wear the uniform because

of a rule that says they must be in uniform to go onto the field to talk with a player or umpire.

The ranks of player-managers dwindled as the game braced for a new on-field management paradigm. Team leaders were soon expected to have specialized field expertise, control over their players, and overall personnel management skills. By the late 1930s, most teams were run by a full-time field manager who wasn't on the team's playing roster. There have been a few other player-managers since then. Notable was the tenure of Mel Ott, a Hall of Fame slugger who managed the New York Giants during the 1940s. The last one to fill the role was Cincinnati's Pete Rose, who transitioned into the team's full-time manager after a couple years. Rose was forced from the latter position amid the gambling controversy that's keeping him out of Cooperstown.

Since the early days, managers have dealt with open revolt, dissension, and disobedience among players. It only got worse when, around the 1930s, baseball stars started to make more money than managers, challenging their authority and team value. It was tough to keep respect among the ranks.

For some managers, a sketchy playing career was a liability. Tony LaRussa played for three teams during his major league career, which began in 1963. He spent most of his professional career in the minors, was an abysmal hitter, and rarely played. Six years after leaving the game, and soon after getting his law degree, LaRussa became the manager for the Chicago White Sox. What could he possibly teach his players? Tort Law? Certainly not how to hit. This was a hurdle that even he recognized, once saying, "The toughest thing for me as a young manager is that a lot of my players saw me play. They know how bad I was."

Free agency added to the cauldron, creating some of the greatest problems for managers since the early 1900s. Starting in the 1980s, players became used to the idea of being not only highly paid, but able to move from team to team. And the intense media scrutiny that accompanied entertainment celebrities also affected baseball players. The team manager not only ran the strategy on the field; he also had to protect his players' reputations. Reporters pestered constantly; some were there to talk about baseball, others appeared to be on a mission to find stories about rich guys acting badly. As if all this isn't enough, today's managers also have to foster relationships with front-office staff and their peers in the stands, the armchair managers.

My college roommate and I went to the Windy City Classic as a graduation present to ourselves. It was a great way to end our college careers, hanging out at the park, as Chicagoans. We rooted for both teams because they were both from Chicago, and so were we. We talked to the fans and watched people get all riled up supporting their "Cubbies" or "Sox." It was a really memorable day. It doesn't matter that I don't even remember who won!

—Vanessa, 28

CHAPTER 16

The Good, the Bad, and the Seemingly Competent

$\mathcal{W}$ith all the hassle, it's amazing that anyone would want to be a baseball manager. Much like contemporary political life, it seems like the ones who are the most qualified wouldn't be interested in the scrutiny and emotional hazard that come with the territory. But this isn't political life, it's baseball. A lot of players still want in on the excitement after they hang up their spikes.

In the early days, owners didn't ask managerial candidates to submit to Rorschach tests to ensure compatibility, so someone seemingly qualified to coach—such as a star player—could be easily miscast in the role. And when this happened, it was nasty. Players threatened mutiny. There were clubhouse screaming matches, front-office screaming matches, vicious firings, sneaky trades, on-field tirades, and a bit of manager versus player fisticuffs. Rogers Hornsby is a good example of a poor hire. The Hall of Fame hitter topped hitting lists during the ten years before becoming the player-manager for the St. Louis Cardinals in 1925. However, the respect

that pitchers gave him at the plate throughout his career wasn't enough to earn him admiration as a manager. His difficult behavior with players and owners was intolerable, and he was traded to the New York Giants after the Cardinals' 1926 championship season. A year later, he was sent packing to Boston, and the year after that he went to the Chicago Cubs. Hornsby stayed put for three years before heading back to St. Louis. Wasn't anyone looking at this guy's job history? Where's a good human resources department when you need one?

Hornsby wasn't the only superstar athlete-turned-management failure. At about the same time that Hornsby was practicing his scorched-earth approach to annoying his various bosses and teammates, other Hall of Famers like Ty Cobb and Walter Johnson were doing their own ineffective two-step in other parts of the league. Years later, even Ted Williams was the beneficiary of an attempted player coup while leading the Washington Senators to a fifth-place finish in 1971. These managers, and others like them, seem to have had a difficult time relating to ordinary human athletes, in terms of ability and fervor. Their inept management of their rank-and-file translated into oodles of lost games.

Though he won the Manager of the Year award in 1969, Williams lost more games than he won in his four years of managing, finishing with a career .429 winning percentage. Hornsby didn't fare much better, finishing up his fifteen-year career with a .463 percentage. Cobb, at least, won more than half of his games, ending with a .519 record. Johnson looks like the tactical genius in this competition; the "Big Train" had ninety-seven wins over the breakeven mark, or a .550 winning percentage during his seven years as a manager.

Not all managers were bad; many were loved as much as Hornsby was loathed. John McGraw is recognized as one of the game's preeminent managers, and he was an average third baseman, with a career batting average of .333, twenty-fourth on the all-time list. It's respectable, but not Hall-of-Fame material. Known for his spunk as a player, he fostered a similar spirit among his players. This extended to creative schemes that would, under normal circumstances, be classified as cheating. No matter. McGraw was loved, and it was all-the-better that he was a big winner. Unlike those other wannabe manager types, McGraw accumulated three World Series rings and seven National League pennants. He also had a .586 winning percentage,

which, over the course of his thirty-three year management career, amounts to 378 games over the 500 mark.

There were also those managers who fit into a leadership role more easily than they fit into the role of player, such as Tony LaRussa. Indeed, some of the game's best managers were never hugely successful in the major leagues, if they even made it that far.

Connie Mack managed for more than fifty years, beginning as a player-manager for Pittsburgh in 1894. As a player he finished his career with a .245 batting average. Nothing remarkable, but he hit his stride during his fifty years managing and retired with 3,731 career wins, more than all major league managers. Mack packed a lot of losses into those years, too, leading his peers in that category, as well.

As a manager, Mack was known as a gentle spirit in the clubhouse. This attitude was in stark contrast to his cheeky trickery as a catcher for three teams from 1886 through 1896. Behind the plate, Mack used to distract opposing teams' batters with chatter and other unsportsmanlike conduct. Once at the helm, however, he toned down his behavior. Eschewing the double-knits, Mack wore a suit in the dugout, never said anything bad in public, and dealt with player issues one-on-one, sometimes over long walks after hours. One way he helped lead his team was to deaden baseballs by freezing them and then sneaking them into the game while his pitchers were on the mound. When the other team's batters hit the deadened balls, they wouldn't travel as far as, say, the *untreated* balls that his team got to whack. And he would sabotage the other team by stationing a drone in centerfield to steal signs from the opposing team. Hey, we said he "toned down" his behavior. We didn't say he became a saint.

Although McGraw's and Mack's numbers as players weren't worthy of Hall of Fame consideration, the 1937 Veterans Committee voted them both into Cooperstown on the merit of their managing.

Joe McCarthy is another such manager who wouldn't be found in the Hall of Fame if it weren't for his talent as a manager. He never even made it to the major leagues, or the "Big Show." Rather, he wallowed in the minors for fifteen years. On April 14, 1914, he was the second batter to face a nineteen-year-old rookie pitcher named Babe Ruth, who was making his professional debut playing for his local minor league team, the International League's Baltimore Orioles. Excitement quickly brewed around Ruth. The

future slugger was snapped up by the Boston Red Sox early that July—just six weeks before the Panama Canal opened for business.

Meanwhile, McCarthy stayed on the sidelines of the growing national pastime until he was recruited to manage the Chicago Cubs before the 1926 season. In 1931 he moved to run the New York Yankees, where Babe Ruth stalked the outfield. Ruth had not only become a mature slugger since he and McCarthy faced off seventeen years earlier, he had also become a household name—and McCarthy was on his way toward becoming one, too. McCarthy managed the Bronx Bombers through May 1946, winning seven World Series with a rotating tap of Hall of Famers such as Joe DiMaggio, Lou Gehrig, Phil Rizzuto, Lefty Gomez, and Ruth. He retired in the middle of the 1950 season with 2,125 wins and a .615 winning percentage, putting him atop the manager totem pole. McCarthy shares the record for most managerial World Series wins with Casey Stengel, who took over the Yankees in 1949.

Once you walk into the stadium, no matter what your age, you feel like you're twelve again. The crack of the bat, the smell of the grass . . . ahhh!

—Anonymous

CHAPTER 17

Sacrifice

*W*hen evaluating the talents of a particular manager, it's important to put his work in context. Baseball isn't divided up into years or decades as much as it is divided up into generations. Joe McCarthy came forth in the midst of the modern game's first power hitting age, when pitchers were reeled in by new rules and the Babe was busy shattering records and streetlights. Gus Schmelz, on the other hand, started his managing career in 1884 when new pitching styles were slowly burying the hitting game.

For instance, during the late 1870s, pitchers were digging the tricky curve ball that Candy Cummings had recently taught them. This new pitch baffled batters. As a result, total runs scored per game hit a low in 1880. Pitchers were getting crafty, and managers needed to take heed. A new form of baseball was on the horizon.

Schmelz was a well-seasoned manager by 1890. This experience helped him be among the first to recognize that, with the new pitcher-based world order, big, sweeping home run swings typically led to Reggie Jackson-esque strikeouts and ordinary fly outs. That was no way for his team to win ballgames. And Schmelz would know, having managed a few different teams to unspectacular finishes. To meet this challenge, he minimized the value of

the home-run swing on his team's repertoire. He popularized various bunt plays as well as perfected the art of hitting behind the runner, a precursor to what fans now recognize as the "hit and run." And he encouraged his players to steal bases so they'd be in better position to score. All of these plays were perfectly suited for teams dependent on speedy runners and contact hitters, rather than lumbering slugger types. This type of baseball is now commonly referred to as "small ball."

The way Schmelz saw it, small ball was a novel strategy that got runners from base to base with small hits, as opposed to big, home-run-garnering blasts. Eventually, these less-spectacular plays got baserunners to second base and in scoring position; most players—especially fast ones—can score from second on a teammate's ordinary, low-risk base hit (a single). These types of hits are more likely with players who are good at making contact with the ball instead of those players who try for fancy, chancy home runs. Before long, other managers were also thinking about how to get their baserunners into scoring position.

One way to advance a runner into scoring position is for the batter to hit a "sacrifice fly," a high fly ball hit purposefully deep to the outfield, ideally ending with the batter being ruled out in exchange for a runner advancing to the next base. Because the ball goes so far, it may look like the batter was trying for a home run. But he wasn't: his goal was to get the runner into scoring position.

The crux of the "sac fly" is that the ball is hit far and high enough that, once it is caught for the predictable out, a runner has enough time to "tag up" and run to the next base safely. This doesn't sound too difficult until you realize that there's a catch—figuratively and literally. When the ball is caught and the batter is out, the runner is free to try to run to the next base. This is risky. The danger is that, as the runner sets out to advance, the fielder will throw the ball to the same base in the hope that his throw will get there before the baserunner, rendering him out. Since the hit to the outfield was caught for the sacrifice out, throwing out the advancing runner would result in two outs, or a double play. Thrilling! However, a sacrifice play is intended to advance the runner, not set him up for failure. Thus, a team likely will only try a sacrifice play like this with a competent baserunner, one who is relatively speedy and isn't likely to get thrown out trying to advance. Lumbering louts need not apply.

In Game Seven of the 1955 World Series against the Yankees, Gil Hodges proved to be an important guy. He drove in the Dodgers' first run in the top of the fourth and hit a sacrifice fly in the sixth inning that allowed Pee Wee Reese to score from third. In fact, after getting on base with a base hit to center field, speedy Reese scurried around the bases by virtue of two bunts, one from Duke Snider and one from Roy Campanella. After getting the team's only two RBI that day (on a single in the fourth and a sacrifice in the sixth), Hodges then caught the last out of the 2-0 game, securing the Dodgers' first World Series Championship.

Hodges sacrificed his chance at glory by hitting a ball that was likely to be caught, resulting in an out for him—in a World Series game, nonetheless! Of course, Hodges got enough glory to satisfy most of us. The play is perfect for contact hitters because sacrifice flies don't require a home run swing, though Hodges had a pretty good one. In fact, a sac fly is relatively easy for contact hitters, and the strikeout risk is lower than it is when a batter tries to swing for the fences. A sacrifice is attempted only when the batter's team has fewer than two outs in the inning. This is because if there are already two outs when a batter hits a long sacrifice ball to the outfield, the caught ball will be the final out of the inning and considered an ordinary fly out, not a graciously executed sacrifice. The runner didn't advance. In fact, since the inning is over, the runner left on base may as well be in Tahiti as in scoring position.

But all of this potential is for naught if the ball doesn't travel far enough before being caught. If this happens, it is a poorly accomplished sac fly and deemed a mere fly out. This means that, not only is the batter out, but the runner doesn't have enough time to beat a throw to the next base. Most savvy runners know their limits and will opt to stay safely on the base. The thrill is gone.

Schmelz also had his team practice sacrifice bunts, a softer version of the sac fly, which is also implemented only when there are fewer than two outs in the inning. A bunt is a relatively easy hitting play when the batter doesn't take a full swing but rather slides his top hand up to about the middle of the bat and leans in to meet the pitch, gently tapping it with the bat. This tactic deadens the trajectory of the ball and, if done well, lays the ball a few yards up either baseline leading to first or third bases, that is, up the foul lines. While the infielders rush toward home plate to field the lifeless

ball, baserunners have a chance to advance. The batter may make a valiant attempt at reaching first base, all the while recognizing that he'll probably be thrown out. Ah, the noble sacrifice. But the play can be dramatic when a really fast runner is the one at the plate. This is because the defense knows the speedster has the ability to make it to first safely. While the runner bears down the ninety feet to first base, the infielders scramble to get the ball, cover the bases, and make the throw; it can become a very close play. The thrill is back!

When a pitcher is in the lineup, he is often called upon to lay down sacrifice bunts. Simply put, most pitchers are lousy hitters, often flirting with the Mendoza Line. If a pitcher tries to hit the ball into play, it will likely end up as an out anyway. With a sacrifice bunt, he can at least put a runner into scoring position.

The scoring position concept was unheard of before Schmelz's smallball concept went mainstream. Heck, before that point, all runners were in scoring position when a home run was hit! This is exactly what Schmelz battled against. In August of 1896, he told the *Washington Post*, "There is room for improvement in the science of batting." He continued, "I have already told the boys that they cannot practice too much in sacrifice hitting. Of course, sacrificing may interfere with a player's batting averages, but I want no player in my team who has a record bee buzzing in his bonnet."

Not only was Schmelz terrifically alliterative, but his pet project was perfectly poised for the league to follow suit. By the mid-1890s, Schmelz's nickel-and-dime approach to baseball was widespread. The concept made it possible for teams with smaller hitters to compete by not relying on home runs but, rather, nipping away at the score, one run at a time. Always have a guy on base, threatening to score. Scoot him around the bases with bothersome bunts and sacrifices. Watch the pitcher sweat. Soon, he'll develop a nasty tick. Who needs someone to wallop a home run when you can psychologically damage opposing players for months? This is so much more enjoyable!

Not only did small ball give new significance to previously undervalued players, it spawned new defensive strategy. These strategies were needed to crush the newfound baserunning power. One of these strategies was having pitchers intentionally walk batters. Walking a batter gives him a free pass to first base. Sometimes teams do this to "set up a double play," which is used when there is a runner on second base and no one on first. A team would

only set up a double play with less than two outs in the inning; otherwise, if there were already two outs, a double play would be overkill. With only a runner on second, an infield ball hit to the shortstop will result in the batter being thrown out at first. One out. The shortstop had to go for the out at first because any smart runner on second base wouldn't budge with the shortstop standing next to him holding the ball. Anyway, that one out would be sufficient when there were already two outs—the batter being thrown out would end the inning.

But if there are less than two outs in the inning, things can be different with that lone runner on second. Defenses will try to increase their chances at getting two outs by setting up the double play. To do this, the pitcher walks the batter to first. Now, there are runners on first and second bases. Let's take that same infield ball hit to the shortstop. The batter hits the ball and starts running to first; the guy on first, who was just intentionally walked, is forced to vacate and run to second. Likewise, the runner on second must leave and go to third. Everyone is forced to run when the ball is hit into play. In this scenario, when the shortstop fields the ball, he may step on second base to get a "force out" on the baserunner who is coming from first (in a force situation, the runner does not need to be tagged with the ball; stepping on the base is enough.) The force at second base is one out. The shortstop will then throw the ball to the first baseman to get the batter out. Two outs. By walking a batter to first, the team set up a double play—via the force out at second base—that wasn't otherwise possible. Remember, the play started with runners on first and second. Both the batter and the runner, who was initially on first, got out. What has become of the baserunner who was on second? That player got to get to third base unimpeded. But that may not matter, anyway. With the double play that just happened, there's a good chance that the inning is over. He can still make that connecting flight to Tahiti.

Or a pitcher may walk a batter because he sees him as a big-hit threat. For instance, a reliable hitter doesn't need to hit a sacrifice to advance the runners. He is capable of making a good hit and scoring the runner even if the runner isn't as far as second base, the traditional scoring position. Or a consistent power hitter could knock a homer over the fence. One way or the other, if the game is close, the manager of the opposing team does not want this hitter to see any good pitches, so the easiest thing to do is to give him nothing to hit at all. No big deal. The hitter gets sent to first and the pitcher

takes his chances with the next batter. Sure, it's a gamble to allow a runner on base. But it was also a gamble to pitch to him. Pick your poison.

Though common now, this practice of avoiding a batter was not well received in the late 1800s. Intentional walks were so unpopular with fans that the league entertained discussions about banning the practice altogether. And the unsporting nature of the intentional walk still warrants heckling from packed stadiums. The taunts stem from the idea that the pitcher is a bit of a coward. But when the game is on the line and there is a power-hitting guy at the plate—or even an average hitter—maybe the sound strategy is to cut your losses, walk the nuisance, and take the jeers. After all, better to put him on first base willingly than to watch him jog the bases flush with home-run glory.

Imagine the conundrum a manager is in when there are three runners on base and the league's living-legend home-run hitter is at the plate. And, just to get all mucky, it's the bottom of the ninth inning, the game is close, and there are two outs. Your team is winning by only two runs. Did we mention that the other team has loaded the bases? Yes? Okay, armchair manager, what do you do?

Walk the bully.

What?! Have you been bunting the ball with your head again?

Well, who knows what you would really do; but this exact scenario played out on May 28, 1998, when the San Francisco Giants faced the Arizona Diamondbacks. The Giants' Barry Bonds was up at bat with two outs and the bases loaded. Arizona manager Buck Showalter ordered his pitcher, Gregg Olson, to walk Bonds. With Bonds sent to first, the runner on third was "walked in" to score. Now Arizona was ahead by only one run.

San Francisco's Brent Mayne came up after Bonds and faced the bases loaded. But he wasn't a feared hitter. In fact, he was an average hitter given only occasional playing time and, just to make matters worse, hadn't hit well that month. Yes, it sounds like we're picking on the guy but, really, it was no secret to Showalter that Mayne hadn't gotten a hit in a handful of bases-loaded situations from the year before, either. And this wasn't his day. Mayne knocked a hard line-drive deep to the right fielder, who caught the ball and dropped to his knees in relief, having made the catch that ended the game.

"I know it was a little unorthodox," Showalter said afterwards. "But I just felt it was the best chance for us to win a baseball game. It was a choice

between one of the great players in the game or a very good player. It was a tough call, but you go with it, and you live with it."

Of course, giving the opposing team a free run is considered if not taboo, then certainly unconventional. But Barry Bonds causes exceptions to be made to many rules.

I like the history and getting to know the players and their quirks. I also enjoy the feel of being at the game on a Sunday afternoon with the sun on your back, a cold beer in the cup holder, and the roar of the crowd.

—Carrie, 35

CHAPTER 18

Kid Gloves

 $\mathscr{A}$ s you'll read in Section Five, "A Schoolboy's Perfect Profession," pitchers require special handling. How well a manager uses, abuses, or massages his pitchers is a common grinding point among some fans, sportswriters, and others tasked with paying attention to such things. Starting in the late 1800s, pitchers' roles began changing significantly, and the changes never ceased. This constant flux created more work for managers. There became the need for pitching rotations and relief pitchers, ice baths, and coddling.

In the game's infancy, teams rarely employed more than a couple of pitchers. By the 1890s, however, some teams had as many as six pitchers. But there were no starters, relievers, or closers. No specialists. There were just pitchers who were expected to start the game and then complete the game. Today's fans may find it unthinkable that pitchers used to finish all nine innings regularly. And pitch into extra innings, if necessary. To give pitchers a rest between games, the manager would rotate through his staff of five or six pitchers, using the same pitcher only every six games or so. This is why pitching staffs are referred to as pitching "rotations."

Managers started to experiment with relief pitchers in the 1930s. Relief pitchers replace the starting pitcher when he becomes fatigued or less effective. When relief pitchers became valuable team assets in the 1950s, managers looked for additional tools to help them use starters and relievers in tandem. Some teams began tracking a starter's "pitch count." Please, don't confuse this with "the count," which tracks balls and strikes during an at bat. The pitch count is the number of pitches a pitcher has thrown during a game. This number helps managers forecast not only when the starter may begin to tire, but also when a reliever might be needed to take over. How do you know when a manager is considering a pitching change? Look to the stadium's bullpen, where pitchers practice and prepare to come into the game. If you see a pitcher and catcher warming up during the game, the manager is considering calling for a replacement.

In 1962, the Los Angeles Dodgers' Don Drysdale won the Cy Young Award, pitching's highest honor. Drysdale pitched before relievers became common in the league, and he completed nineteen of the forty-one games he started that year. This means he pitched from start to finish, no matter how many innings were needed to complete the game. The twenty-five-year-old starter also faced an exhausting 1,289 batters during 314 innings, both workhorse league records that year. Just to show how things changed, more than three decades later, Atlanta's John Smoltz scored his own Cy Young Award. He completed six of his thirty-five starts in 1996, facing 995 batters in 254 innings. Drysdale looks like an Iron Man by comparison. That is, until you look further back. In 1904, the then-thirty-seven-year-old Cy Young started forty-one games, just like Drysdale did in '62. However, Young finished all but one of his starts and faced 1,475 batters in 380 innings. Who's a tough guy, now?

But this isn't yet another tired discourse about how the game has changed, how pitchers battled it out, and how they became the divas of the dugout. Nowadays, managers must use their discretion to decide how many pitches their starter throws during a game. It is a tenuous science. Remember, pitchers are fragile. Not wimpy, per se, just delicate. Their arms take a beating and require sufficient rest.

In 2006, Seattle Manager Mike Hargrove didn't want his twenty-year-old phenom, Felix Hernandez, to wear out his arm early in his career. So, he treated the youngster very gently, limiting Hernandez to about 100 pitches per game, a customary benchmark for contemporary starters, and to no

more than 200 total innings during the season. Still, Hernandez didn't fare terribly well that season; nor did his team.

Like Hargrove, team managers work to tame and mold the team's prized pitching resource. Proper management of throwing arms, bone-heads and other appendages can prolong careers and win championships. But sometimes prolonged careers and championships aren't in the cards. Billy Martin is widely credited with single-handedly ruining the careers of his entire Oakland five-man starting-pitching rotation while managing the team for three years, beginning in 1980. That first year, Martin's start-ers pitched a combined ninety-three complete games. But, while Martin may have pushed his starters, he couldn't push his team into the playoffs; the Oakland team finished second in the division, fourteen games behind Kansas City, whose five starters completed a total of thirty-seven games.

Oakland's Rick Langford, the twenty-eight-year-old veteran of Martin's staff, contributed twenty-eight complete games and a total of 290 innings that year, by far more than anyone in the American League.

So, Billy Martin overworked his starters. Or so the story goes. Was it all a tyrannical and unnurturing environment? Mike Norris, one of "Martin's Five," was the second-place finisher for the 1980 Cy Young Award. The following year under Martin's tutelage, Norris' teammate, Steve McCatty, was also runner-up for the trophy. That's good recognition for spectacular years, even if the two were exhausted from pitching too frequently. Pleasant anecdotes aside, all five of Martin's starters were out of the league or limp-ing along by 1986. As a rotation, their effectiveness died out soon after the 1980 season.

Many fans have heard some rendition of the baseball saying: "Pitching wins championships." The phrase seems to be overused. You'll likely hear it several times during a season and twice as much during October, when it is championship time. The idea that a team needs strong pitching to defeat championship-caliber opposing teams is probably why managers spend so much energy tending to their starting lineups and preserving their arms and minds for a fruitful playoff run.

Someone may want to question Sparky Anderson about that. Anderson managed the Cincinnati Reds throughout much of the 1970s, winning two World Series and a couple extra NL penants before heading to Detroit. His offensive weaponry in Cincinnati included Pete Rose and future Hall of Famers Joe Morgan, Johnny Bench, and Tony Perez. By the end of the

1975 season, the team's offense outscored every other team in the league by more than 100 runs, and the Reds went on to its first of two consecutive World Series victories, beating the Boston Red Sox, four games to three.

But bats and defense are only supposed to get teams to the playoffs; they are not supposed to win them, and this is where the old saying about pitching comes in. Anderson and the Reds accomplished great things with a rotation of six no-name starters buttressed by a powerful team of relief pitchers; his rotation of virtual nobodies meant there were no outrageous egos to soothe or precious arms to nurse. Because of this, he was free to pull his starters early and often, earning the nickname "Captain Hook" for this willingness. Combined, the 1975 starters logged only twenty-two complete games. Gary Nolan, their best pitcher, pitched only five complete games out of his thirty-two starts, amounting to 210 total innings. Do the math; he was no Big Kahuna. But having starting pitchers complete games was becoming rare in MLB, and Anderson adapted by using his relievers without apology. The year before, the Los Angeles Dodgers' Mike Marshall became the first reliever to win the Cy Young. Change was afoot, and Anderson helped the cause.

There is the task of managing pitchers throughout the course of a season or a career, and then there is the task of managing pitchers throughout a game. Sometimes this entails keeping starters in the game, even though fans and sports writers may vilify this choice. Sometimes it entails taking a pitcher out of the game, even though fans and sports writers may vilify this choice as well.

In Game Seven of the spectacular 2003 American League playoffs, Boston's Grady Little made a managerial decision that left Red Sox Nation reeling. In this dramatic rubber match, the Yankees' Roger Clemens pitched poorly and was pulled in the fourth inning. But things were going well for the Red Sox and their starter, Pedro Martinez. He had thrown 100 pitches through seven innings and the Sox were winning, 5-2. By the beginning of the eighth inning, many Red Sox fans thought it was time to replace Pedro. But manager Little kept Martinez in the game. The short story is that Martinez struggled. He was yanked after his next twenty-three pitches allowed the "Damn Yankees" to tie the game, which was eventually sent into extra innings, and ended in the bottom of the eleventh inning when New York's uncelebrated hitter Aaron Boone homered to win the game. Fans went wild. Bret Boone, Aaron's big brother and the Seattle Mariners'

second baseman, was on hand that night as a guest television announcer. Cameras caught Bret wiping away tears when Aaron was swarmed by teammates as he jumped on home plate.

Few managers manipulated their pitching staff as well as Paul Richards, who led the Chicago White Sox and Baltimore Orioles during his twelve-year career. On May 15, 1951, the rookie White Sox manager was worried how his reliever, righty Harry Dorish, would fare against one of the league's best hitters, lefty Ted Williams, who had hit his 300th career home run earlier in the game and made sport of toying with the league's right-handed pitchers. Now, with a close game in the eighth inning, Richards wasn't going to sit around to find out how this match up would pan out. As Williams prepared to take his position at the plate, Richards pulled his third baseman out of the game and moved Dorish, the pitcher(!), to play third. Then he brought in lefty pitcher Billy Pierce to face Williams. The scheme worked. The Hall of Fame hitter popped up for an out and Pierce, having done what he was called in to do, hit the showers. Dorish returned to the mound to pitch to the next guy, and another third baseman was put into the game. The White Sox won the game in the eleventh inning, 9-7.

When Richards was asked afterwards whether he was worried that Dorish, the pitcher(!), would have to field a ball at third base, he replied. "Well, no. I'd never seen Williams hit a ball to the third baseman," referring to Williams' tendency to hit to the other side of the field. Richards used this switch again a couple times in the next two years and set the stage for the renaissance of the "double switch." The double switch is an old-school management play that is used when the manager is trying to avoid having his pitcher bat. The ploy is still seen in the National League. The double-switch is somewhat intriguing, indeed, but we are not going to delve into it. That would involve charts, sharpened pencils, and little standup figures to do it justice. A couple shots of whiskey wouldn't hurt, either. But we are running out of both pencils and whiskey, and we still haven't talked about the infield fly rule. Better make another, er, "supply" run!

When it's time to pull the pitcher, whether he's reached his preordained "pitch count" or if he's just stinking up the joint, there will be a mound visit. This is when the manager visits the mound and takes the ball from the pitcher, the universal signal for "you're done." The pitcher may head back to the dugout alone or stand on the mound and wait for the replacement to

show up. Then the manager hands the ball to the relief pitcher. The game continues.

It sounds so civil. And it often looks that way. But Sparky Anderson, who knew it wasn't always a terribly polite encounter, would walk to the mound with his head down. "I know I am not happy to be going there, and I know he isn't happy to see me," Anderson told the *Sporting News* in 1994. "I have one rule. When I put out my hand, put the ball in. Jack Morris [a starter for Detroit] would see how many blood vessels he could break, banging it in there."

My favorite baseball memory is from Father's Day, sometime in the mid-'60s. My family had field seats on the third-base line, it was a sunny and warm Los Angeles Sunday afternoon, [and] I wore a yellow cap (my favorite at the time) and my Spaulding Carl Yastrzemski glove. I don't remember if we saw Koufax or Drysdale pitch, but I remember that as one of the most wonderful days of my nine-year-old life.

—Nancy, 52

CHAPTER 19

A Critic by Any Other Name

There is some debate as to whether managers and their decisions are meaningful in the scope of an entire season. You may have heard a drunken fan who thinks he can do the job calling for the pitcher's head from the centerfield bleachers. Many others think they'd like a shot at the position. Hence, the flurry of "Fantasy Leagues," where anyone can run his own ball club. Glory, at last! Or, bust.

We like to think managers are useful. After all, they are the butt of so much contempt that it would be folly to spend so much time grousing about them if they didn't matter.

Some researchers have spent perhaps too much time trying to figure out whether managerial judgments are constructive. They've dissected decisions, input some rootin' tootin' algorithms, replayed games on computers, and come up with interesting theories. One of their conclusions is that "small ball" strategy calls (that is, when to bunt, steal, or swing) have little sway on a game's outcome. Another conclusion is that treating pitchers kindly helps teams win. Okay, managers, send your pitchers flowers, and don't try too much fancy stuff—next debate.

If it were only that easy.

Managers are involved with their coaches and players at varying levels. Some managers prefer minimal interaction with their players. Others, like the White Sox's Ozzie Guillen, use the hands-on approach. He can be seen teaching, talking, and laughing with his players. You may also see him engage in forehead-busting, water-bottle-throwing tirades.

What most everyone agrees on is that it is the manager's responsibility to have his players ready to play. This is the big intangible that has the most bearing on games won or lost. In some cases, it is really not too different from how the manager of a fast food joint schedules his personnel. He knows to staff the graveyard shift with someone who oversleeps and is chronically late when it comes to opening shop in the morning.

One of the manager's most important roles is to decipher the puzzle of how to make the team perform best: which players are in the best frame of mind, who is feeling lucky, or who has the best talent to face the upcoming opponent?

Sometimes managerial decisions have no basis in rational thought. In August, 1929, Connie Mack's Philadelphia A's were on the way to the World Series, having led the league since mid-May. Mack was on the verge of cutting one of his old backup pitchers from the team, thirty-five-year old Howard "Bob" Ehmke, who had started only eight games that season. As the manager was informing the pitcher of his decision, Ehmke threw Mack a curveball. He said, "Mr. Mack, there is one great game left in this old arm." Instead of sorely accepting his fate and skulking out of town, Ehmke tried to convince Mack to play him in the upcoming World Series against the Chicago Cubs, even though Mack already had a fine starting pitching rotation. Sounds like someone was sniffing a little fantasy baseball, doesn't it? Inexplicably, Mack decided to go with Ehmke in Game One of the Series.

Ehmke delivered. He pitched a complete game win and set a World Series record with thirteen strikeouts. Cy Young, long retired from the game, said that Ehmke's game was one of the "grandest displays" he'd seen. But how did Mack know that Ehmke was going to come through for the team? He did what managers do best: knowing their players and knowing when they can be expected to perform. The information isn't found on stat

sheets. It is an art of playing hunches that can befuddle critics and infuriate ledger-toting assistants.

There may be some debate about various calls, but when it comes time to talk to the umpire, no one is better suited than the manager. After all, it is for these moments that he dons the double-knits, granting him the power to walk onto the field. Conversations with umpires can vary from subdued to downright juvenile. Some skippers are good at the art of persuasion, getting umpires to discuss and, possibly reverse, a questionable call. Sometimes a manager only has to remind the umpire of the rulebook. Or, as the Orioles' Earl Weaver once did, defiantly tear up the rulebook.

Historically, an inaccurately or inconsistently called strike zone has often been a point of contention between batters and umpires. It is up to the umpire's judgment as to whether a pitch passed through the strike zone or not. Technology fueled the inferno when television stations began airing video representations of the strike zone—and where pitches were thrown in relation to the strike zone. Now, with the new technology, "No way! That was low and outside!" can be yelled with a modicum of accuracy from fans watching the game from their living room couches in Chattanooga, where the nearest MLB strike zone is 130 miles away.

Before long MLB adopted "QuesTec," a technology that helps umpires call a consistent strike zone. Umpires review the QuesTec videotaped information post-game and evaluate themselves on how well they called the games. In 2007, MLB said umpires averaged 95-percent accuracy in calling the strike zone. However, until something else develops in this realm, calling strike zones remains a judgment call—and one that is not to be trifled with.

Sometimes managers' outbursts get them ejected from games. When this happens, they must leave the field and the dugout, making it nearly impossible for them to manage their players. Most are undeterred by an expulsion. Some try to watch on TVs in the locker room and issue strategy from the shadows of the tunnel leading to the dugout. There are reports of ejected managers coming back as groundskeepers, fans, or members of the press. Some try disguises, such as when Mets manager Bobby Valentine briefly reappeared in the dugout after an ejection wearing a faux mustache and dark glasses.

Baltimore Orioles manager Earl Weaver considered quarrelling with the umpire pure sport. He was ejected almost 100 times during the course of

his seventeen-season career. In August, 1975, he was ejected from both games of a double header. It is well known that Weaver had a long-standing feud with umpire Ron Luciano. In the minors, he was ejected in four consecutive games by Luciano. When they both got to the majors, Luciano tossed Weaver eight times. The rift was so bad that eventually the ump was not assigned to any more Orioles games. It's possible that Weaver was right to argue calls. In one of Luciano's books, *The Umpire Strikes Back*, he wrote that "any umpire who claims he has never missed a play is, well, an umpire." Luciano seemed to believe that ignorance really was bliss.

Sometimes successfully managing a team means simply holding your tongue. In 1987, when the often-vocal Lou Piniella was managing the Yankees, he may have helped his team by just keeping quiet, but certainly this was not out of self-restraint. New York was playing in Los Angeles and leading the game, 1-0. Pitching the game were two players known for their craftiness and trickery, Tommy John for the Yankees and Don Sutton for the Angels. According to Bill Madden's book, *Damned Yankees*, television cameras showed Sutton in the Angels' dugout taking sandpaper out of his pocket during the third inning. Since roughing up the surface of a baseball is a form of cheating, Yankee owner George Steinbrenner was incensed to see this. He called Piniella to ask what the manager intended to do about Sutton "doctoring" the ball. Referring to the fact that the Yankees were winning, Piniella told his boss that he wasn't planning on busting Sutton and getting him thrown out of the game. "What it means, George," Piniella said, "is that our guy is cheating better than their guy."

I didn't get hooked on baseball until I became a mom. I remember my son's first T-ball game thirty-five years ago, when one of his teammates swung a bat at the ball and immediately began running—toward third base. His dad was mortified, but the mothers in the crowd laughed with joy and cheered.

—Jeannie, 57

SECTION FOUR

Assume the Position

When a batter awaits a pitch, eight opponents face him, trying to keep him off the bases. If that's not bad enough, there is one more player behind him, crouched down as if to hide. Yes, lest you be tricked, this guy is in cahoots with the rest of them. A daunting hurdle? Indeed. In football, you have eleven players trying to keep eleven others from scoring. Ditto for soccer. In basketball, it's five against five. Cricket players face similar odds as baseball players. But, as you know, the games are so different that you shouldn't even start to think that they are in any way related. There is a whole commission that will come and get you. Baseball has nasty odds.

Now all eyes are on the batter because he is faced with this seemingly lopsided and unfair challenge. Specifically, the batter is facing the above-referenced fielders, otherwise known as the opposing team's defenders. These guys are known as the "position players." And don't forget about the sneaky one behind home plate; his code name is "the catcher," and he's the brains of the operation.

The nine of them may look like a menacing bunch, and this perception has merit. But they are crying inside. The torment they shoulder is inconceivable to most normal folks. Sure these guys make good plays—often amazing plays that are viewed thousands of times on cable sports channels. But just as often, fielders are remembered for their mistakes or often embarrassing plays, which land them on the blooper video instead of the highlights reel. It is the age-old story of the one that got away. Or the one that bounced off his head.

CHAPTER 20

Wake Me When It's Over

*A*s we noted in Chapter 14, "Run Like You Mean It," baseball is often recognized as a game of hitting, not running. But it is an atrocity to ignore a great runner like Pete Rose who added so much excitement to a game with his patented lunch-pail hustle. And a century later, baseball pundits still talk about how Ty Cobb was a terror around the basepaths. Someone is paying attention.

Much the same can be said of fielding. Like its scarcely more attractive half-sister, the running game, most statistics ignore fine defensive play. The acrobatic diving play and ensuing throw from the belly that beats the runner to first and earned an out? Yawn. But, seriously, the guy who made this play would at least get notice from the unpaid intern in the press box who is tasked with logging underappreciated statistics. The intern would mark down the play in the player's "A" column. Other than being short for "A real player hits home runs," this is the abbreviation for "assist," which

means that the fielder licking his wounds from making a spectacular play is credited with assisting his team in making an out.

For more than fifty years, these mostly defensive guys had to rejoice silently because everyone laughed at them for celebrating something as mundane as a making a catch. In 1957 baseball decided it was time to recognize its defenders. Though the award system and its criteria have changed throughout the years, coaches and managers in each league now vote on who gets the Gold Glove at each position for their respective leagues. This is the case for all positions except the outfield. Instead of presenting a Gold Glove award for each outfield position—right, center, and left—three outfielder Gold Glove awards are presented each year for each league. This leaves open the chance that three center fielders will win the award, which happens often enough because these talented athletes are popular guys.

Ozzie Smith was a popular guy, although he wasn't a center fielder; he was a star defenseman who won thirteen consecutive Gold Gloves while playing shortstop for the San Diego Padres and St. Louis Cardinals during the 1980s and 1990s. Not surprisingly, Smith was an average hitter and rarely hit for power, knocking only twenty-eight balls over the fence in his nineteen-year career—not bad for a shortstop. This is often how it goes for defensive masters. And, as it turns out, he was a pretty good baserunner, too. A fielder *and* a runner?! That's the *coup de grace* of underrated talents. It's amazing this guy could afford to feed his family. But all the diving catches in the world didn't compare to what the Hall of Famer identified as one of his greatest baseball moments: when he hit one of those scant few homers in the bottom of the ninth to win Game Five of the 1985 National League division championship. Dude! Don't let them know you care!

An interesting transformation occurs when players assume their positions on the field. Before becoming "defenders," players appear to be just a group of big clunky fellows trying, one by one, to hit a ball. It is when they take the field that it becomes clear how they move together as a team. The choreography in the field is set to the rhythm of the batter and pitcher. Just watch the fielders for a few innings, and you too can learn their moves. If a right-handed hitter is at bat, fielders may shimmy to the left since righties tend to pull the ball to the third base side of the field. A home-run hitter? The three outfielders will slide back toward the outfield fence so they are better positioned to catch a long fly ball.

Back in the mid-1900s, Ted Williams' extraordinary hitting ability frustrated teams. His prowess with the bat inspired the "Williams Shift," a defensive maneuver invented by Cleveland player-manger Lou Boudreau to defuse the hitter's dominance. This is also sometimes referred to as the "Boudreau Shift," for obvious reasons. Noticing that Williams pulled the ball more than other lefties, landing most of his hits to the right of center field, Boudreau dramatically shifted his defense so that only the left fielder was to the left of the pitcher's mound. Everyone else was conspicuously gathered on the other side of the field. Mostly due to this ploy, Williams batted only .200 during Boston's 1946 World Series loss to St. Louis, whose manager had borrowed the idea from Boudreau. Sadly, this trip to the World Series was Williams' only opportunity to win a Championship during his nineteen-year career. In 1967, seven years after Williams retired, the Boston Red Sox appeared in the World Series and lost, again, to the St. Louis Cardinals.

Living in Illinois just across the river from the St. Louis Cardinals (the greatest team in the United States), you just had to be a fan or else you were not normal. In the Catholic grade school I attended from about 1963 to 1971, when the Cardinals were in the World Series, they would wheel a television in the classroom so we could watch the games! Awesome! How could you not like baseball when it allowed you to get out of school work?!

—Wendy, 48

CHAPTER 21

The Catcher and the Horn

*T*he nine field positions have corresponding numbers that are used for recording the game on a scorecard. Announcers and fans also use the position numbers to describe different plays on the field. For instance, a traditional double play that involves the shortstop (position number 6), the second baseman (4), and the first baseman (3) is called a "6-4-3" double play. Those positions make up much of the "horn," which is better known as the infield. More specifically, it is the curved dirt path from first through third base.

The number-one position is the pitcher (1). The next section, "A School Boy's Perfect Profession," is all about pitchers because, well, they are special. This is not news to any of them. So, here, we will deal solely with the team's "position players," covered in numerical order. The position players are the catcher, the first baseman, the second baseman, the third baseman, the shortstop, the left fielder, the center fielder, and the right fielder. Our tour of these positions will start with the number-two fielder, the catcher (2).

He is the shifty one behind the batter who lobs hand signals to the pitcher and runs the defense telepathically, much like *M*A*S*H*'s Radar O'Reilly. Catchers are often the most knowledgeable on the team when it comes to strategy and exposing a batter's Achilles heel.

Catchers have their weak spots, too. It is just that they get to wear the baseball equivalent of body armor to protect themselves from some of the physical danger that accompanies the position. Specifically, the numerous balls that are prone to being fouled off into their chests, faces, and legs. Also, catchers are a team's last-ditch effort at keeping a runner from scoring. Unless it's a bases-loaded situation, as a runner heads to home plate the catcher has to make the tag to get the runner out. Not only is this tag important because it could keep a team from scoring, it is different from any other tag in baseball. In many cases, runners who know they are about to be tagged for an out give up gracefully; they are not permitted to barrel into ball-wielding fielders in an effort to knock the ball loose and onto the ground, negating the tag and, thus, the out—no ball, no tag. But runners heading home are permitted to plow into catchers who are blocking the path to the plate. Good thing there's body armor. When the runner arrives, he tries to dislodge the ball and maybe even the catcher's kidneys, using nothing but the brute force of his elbows. These plays result in some grotesque hits. We think that calling this play a "tag" is a misplaced euphemism, or simply someone's idea of a bad joke. If the bases are loaded, the play at home is a force out and the catcher needs only to step on the plate for the out, a far less hazardous play.

Nineteen-year-old Johnny Bench was called up from the minors to play catcher for the Cincinnati Reds on August 28, 1967. He played in all but a few of that season's remaining games, effectively replacing the team's starting catcher, All-Star Johnny Edwards, who was traded to St. Louis in the following off-season. So, by the beginning of the 1968 season, Bench had won the starting catcher's job. By the end of that season, he had won the National League's Rookie of the Year award. By the end of his seventeen-year career—all with the Reds—he had earned two MVPs, ten Gold Gloves, and fourteen trips to the All-Star game. But all this came with a price. The Hall of Famer's dedication to the position led to a multitude of injuries too depressing to enumerate because sometimes, when all else seemed well, his armor failed him. He reportedly had to replace seven protective cups during his years behind the plate. These cups are used to

keep a player's testicles from rupturing if hit by a hard, rapidly moving object, such as a 90-mph fastball. After retiring, Bench became a professional bowler, although he still got calls from the local opera company, who were looking for a soprano.

A catcher's greatest strength is his arm, which prevents runners from stealing bases and getting into better scoring position. A quality catcher like Bench or Ivan Rodriguez, who spent most of his productive years with the Texas Rangers, is able to thwart many stolen base attempts by catching the pitch and instantly throwing the runner out before the runner reaches the next base. Successful assists like these take a strong and accurate throwing arm. And, to match wits against his running rival, a catcher's instincts must be equally sharp. Few things can stop a great runner from stealing a base, but even super-fast superstars think twice when there is someone behind the plate with a gun for an arm. Middling runners likely will not even try.

Conversely, a catcher's weakness can also be his arm. A bad throwing arm can make it difficult for him to keep runners from stealing bases. This quickly becomes a glaring defensive hole that astute offenses delight in exposing. For instance, in June, 1907, the Washington Senators snickered their way to thirteen stolen bases on catcher Branch Rickey en route to a 16-5 rout over the Yankees. Mets catcher Mike Piazza made public his noodle arm in the early part of the 2002 season when he allowed fifty-one straight runners to steal against him, starting on April 9 and ending on June 16, when he finally caught up with the Yankees' speedy Alfonso Soriano. But Piazza's defensive ineffectiveness didn't jeopardize his job security. The player formally known as the "Mustached Morsel" was a successful hitter and adored by fans. Damn that razor.

While the catcher can be seen as the steady sultan of the plate, the guy playing the field's number-three position, or first base (3), may be regarded as the team ambassador. When runners from opposing teams get a hit that lands them on first base, the runner and first baseman often can be seen chatting and generally yukking it up. Sometimes the first base coach gets in on the action. What could they be talking about? What happened to fierce competitiveness and cutthroat contempt for one's opponent?

In a 2002 interview with *Baseball Digest*, Steve Lyons, who, by the way, played for five different teams and logged time at every position, including pitcher, between 1985 and 1993, talked about how first basemen are

the social hub of a team and how, when he got on base, he would have assignments for the fielder. "I'd be like, 'OK, we got three or four guys on the team that are cowboys, so we need a cowboy bar. And we need a jazz bar, and we need a metal bar. Next time I get here you need to have three or four ideas for where to go tonight." It was unlikely that Lyons, a hitter with a mediocre .252 batting average, would get back to first base that day, which poses a few unfortunate problems. The most glaring issue being the off-chance that some cowboys were let loose on the regular world. Or worse, Boston. That is just irresponsible.

Some first basemen take the role of team consul very seriously. Rafael Palmeiro, whose native language is Spanish, learned how to say "You're the man" in Japanese so he would have something to say to Seattle's Ichiro Suzuki when this brilliant hitter inevitably visited the Texas Rangers' turf at first base.

First basemen, as a collection, also are historically the least athletic player on the team. This comes with some strong evidence—namely, John Kruk, who played nearly ten years at the position, starting in 1985. Kruk's slovenly appearance and aloof demeanor fueled the percepton that athletic ability wasn't a prerequisite for the position. And he clearly thought that baseball, in general, didn't take much effort. This attitude was cemented when he told a fan, "I ain't an athlete, lady. I'm a baseball player." This story has a number of renditions, but Kruk's own version, as printed in his book, *I Ain't An Athlete, Lady . . .* says that the woman chastised him for smoking and drinking and, generally, not treating his body the way she thought athletes were supposed to.

While there are have been plenty of first basemen like John Kruk—most without the "Lovable Lout" attitude—statisticians recently came up with new ways to measure the defensive deftness of first basemen. One of these is to record the number of times the fielder saves a bad throw. This statistic is called "bad throw saves," which isn't particularly creative but, nor, it can be argued, are many statisticians. A fielder gets a bad throw save when he is able to rein in other fielder's throws that are off target. The target, incidentally, is the first baseman's glove, or somewhere within reasonable reach of the glove. This ability can turn would-be errors (on the fielder who made the throw) into outs. In this way, first basemen can keep runners off base; they also can make their teammates look good by saving them the embarrassment of having made a possible, and possibly costly, error.

Most baseball experts agree that St. Louis slugger Albert Pujols is the best defensive first baseman to have played in a long time. The 2001 Rookie of the Year is particularly adroit at "saving" balls, yet he's won only one Gold Glove, in 2006, while three have gone to Derrek Lee, who has played eleven seasons at first, beginning in 1997. What gives? Maybe the Gold Glove award is a popularity contest, after all.

This idea—and the rivalry between the two fielders—was first pronounced during the Gold Glove voting for 2005. That year Pujols kept forty-two runners from reaching first base because of his ability to corral bad throws from other fielders. This didn't gain him enough notice, however, to win the league's defensive award for first base. The National League's managers and coaches instead bestowed the first baseman's Gold Glove distinction to Lee, who had only six errors that year. That was eight less than Pujols, but Lee made about half as many of those sexy "saves." Not to be outdone, Pujols took his impressive offensive stats and snagged that year's MVP. So there.

Despite this new brand of statistic, it is true that the nature of the position doesn't require much in the way of athleticism. Usually, first basemen are put into the spot because they are capable of making big hits when it's their turn to come up to bat. These are guys like Houston's Jeff Bagwell, who has one Gold Glove to his name and 449 home runs; or San Francisco Giants slugger Willie McCovey, who has no Gold Gloves on his mantle but hit 521 homers over his twenty-two seasons, which he began in 1959 when he won the National League's Rookie of the Year. Hall of Famer Lou Gehrig is another; even though he won no Gold Gloves—he retired eighteen years before the Gold Glove was first awarded—Gehrig is often regarded as the best first baseman ever to play the game. Like many other first basemen, much of his notoriety is based on powerful offensive numbers—493 homers and a .632 slugging percentage, for starters. Gehrig is also famous for his dedication to the sport, amassing 2,130 consecutive games over fifteen years, and for his tragically abbreviated career, which was cut short by the disease that later bore his name.

The number-four position on the field is the second baseman (4), who is positioned in the dirt between first and second base or even a few steps back into the grass toward right field. The second baseman needs to be particularly agile in order to scoop up ground balls, make quick throws to first, and cover a large territory that includes shallow right field and

even first base when the first baseman rushes toward the plate to field a bunt. He also needs nimble feet in order to pivot and make the throw to first in order to turn a double play. Typically, these fielders are not a feared offensive force—their worth to the team is in the defense. We emphasize "typically." Rod Carew slapped the ball to seven batting titles, five of which were earned while playing second base for the Minnesota Twins during the 1970s. However, a need to shore up the team's defense factored into the Hall of Famer's move to first base in 1976.

The Pirates' Bill Mazeroski is a different matter altogether. Sure, he's known, at least to us, for a shocking ninth-inning walk-off home run to win the 1960 World Series over the Yankees. He also played a little field. Well, a lot of it. Mazeroski won the Gold Glove at second for most of the 1960s and, making that World Series homer all the more extraordinary, he never led the league in any offensive statistic. Well, that's unless you include the year the Hall of Fame second baseman led the league in receiving intentional walks. Now, *that's* offensive.

Able or not, the second baseman is primarily responsible for thwarting the "hit and run," which is an offensive play that has its roots in the work of small ball pioneer Gus Schmelz in the late 1880s. Things haven't really changed since then. The hit and run requires a particularly fast runner on first base and an accurate contact hitter at the plate. This strategy could really be called the "run and hit" because the baserunner on first starts running with the pitch, much like he's trying to steal a base. One of the differences between the two plays, however, is that the batter in a hit and run situation doesn't let the ball pass him. Rather, this batter is expected to place a hit past the second baseman and into right field. That's some precision hitting! When the ball is hit as expected, the runner who started on first easily continues to third base by virtue of the long and difficult throw necessary from right field as well as the substantial head start he got from first base by running with the pitch. The batter, meanwhile, is expected to reach first without too much difficulty, but a good second baseman is not supposed to let the ball get through in the first place.

The number five spot is considered the "hot corner" because screaming line drives from right-handed batters often bear down on the third baseman (5). He has to be fearless. Some of these line drives require the third baseman to make athletic diving catches followed by Herculean throws to first from his knees. Fortunately, because the ball gets there so quickly

off the bat, the third baseman normally has a little more time to ensure an accurate throw. Many third basemen have translated their great throwing strength into strength at the plate. This can be seen by the many hard-hitting players at that position.

The Orioles' third baseman Brooks Robinson was a sixteen-time Gold Glove winner. He was so adept at vacuuming up infield ground balls that his opponents in the 1970 World Series nicknamed him "Hoover." After Baltimore won that series, Cincinnati Reds manager Sparky Anderson joked about Robinson's skill, saying, "If I dropped this paper plate, he'd pick it up on one hop and throw me out at first."

When you hear an announcer refer to an "around the horn" double play, it typically involves the third baseman (5) fielding the ball and throwing it to second to get the runner coming from first. The second baseman (4) steps on the base for the force out. That's one out. Then, the second baseman makes the throw to the first baseman (3) to get the batter bearing down on first base. That is two outs. Using the numbers, as you'll often hear, it would be called a "5-4-3 double play." It's rarely as easy as it sounds, especially since the second baseman often has to jump up in the air to avoid a collision from the incoming baserunner, who is trying to distract the second baseman enough to make a bad throw to first. A bad throw may allow his teammate, the batter, to get on base safely.

While we now have traveled around the horn, we haven't finished with the infield. There is still the shortstop, who is often the most heralded infielder on the team. Recently, as often as we read about their talent on the field, a few celebrity shortstops are making headlines based on who their friends are, where their house is, or how they spend the stupid amounts of money they make. Oh, wait. Alex Rodriguez isn't a shortstop, anymore.

The shortstop (6) is a team's primary defense against right-handed hitters, who tend to cut line drives between second and third base. Since the number-six position mirrors the position taken by the second baseman (4), he needs all the same skills as his teammate, and then some, specifically a stronger throwing arm. Because of the frequent action he gets from righties, which is the majority of hitters in the league, he gets more fielding opportunities than anyone else on the team.

Before the 1980s most shortstops were, like second basemen, valued purely for their defense. Not that there was any choice in the matter. With rare exception, most shortstops were lousy hitters, choosing to

swap practice time in the batting cage for the chance to perfect feline-like, midair snatches and diving catches or work toward slivering milliseconds off their throws to first base.

Ozzie Smith owned the gap between second and third. He was also, somewhat oddly, a proponent of pre-game back flips, which did nothing for his hitting game. But none of that seemed to matter. Smith was known as "The Wizard" in the field. He would likely have played every game even if he only hit his weight, which was about 155 pounds. That would be hitting well below the Mendoza line, or .200, as you may recall. Fortunately, his manager didn't have to make that choice. Though not Ruthian, Smith averaged .262 during the span of his career. At his Hall of Fame induction in 2002 he said that he hoped the plaques of more defensive players would fill the halls of Cooperstown.

In 1981 Cal Ripken, Jr., burst onto the infield scene. His appearance broke the mold of typical shortstops with his six-foot, four-inch frame carrying about fifty pounds more than Smith's and many of their contemporaries. Ripken's size created a force with the bat that hadn't been seen in a shortstop since Ernie Banks in the 1950s or Honus Wagner, a big hitter in the early 1900s.

While many shortstops are still small and quick, Ripken paved the way for a lineup of comparatively beefy and big-hitting shortstops such as Nomar Garciaparra, Derek Jeter, and Alex Rodriguez, who gave up playing shortstop with the Texas Rangers for a chance to play for the Yankees, where the team captain, Jeter, was already playing shortstop. Instead, Rodriguez took the open spot at third. As good as Rodriguez and Jeter are at shortstop, Omar Vizquel shut the duo out of many American League Gold Gloves by snagging eleven between 1993 and 2007; in addition, Vizquel also has a respectable career batting average of .274.

If you are ever found muttering to yourself about the infield fly rule, you can bill an infielder for your psychiatry bills. This rule was created because of naughty but astute infielders. In the late 1800s, an infielder would occasionally pretend to catch a pop up and then let it drop to the ground. The only time that this made any sense, as you'll soon read, is when there were runners on *at least* first and second base and less than two outs in the inning. Those conditions are worth remembering. See, if the infielder had merely caught the ball, as he was supposed to, the runners would have simply stayed on base; the caught ball is the sole out. But when the infielder

dropped the ball in the same type of situation (less than two outs with runners on at least first and second), the runners were in a fix—or, rather, a force. Specifically, as soon as the infielder let the ball drop, runners on first and second were forced to go to the next base. But there was never any chance of anyone making it safely. There just wasn't enough time. This is because the guy with the ball was, well, *right there*. The shrewd infielder would throw to the third baseman, who stepped on the base before the runner from second got there for the force, earning one out. Then the third baseman threw the ball to second base to get the force on the runner coming from first; getting two outs, when only one should have happened (the caught ball).

Baseball created the infield fly rule because of these shenanigans. Now, if an umpire thinks the fielder can reasonably be expected to catch the pop up with the preordained conditions in place, the infield fly rule comes into play. This means that the umpire assumes the ball will be caught and calls the batter out before the fielder gets the chance to pull a fast one—or a dropped one. The runners stay on base and complete dinner plans with the first baseman. Everyone's happy.

Wow. Don't worry. Even experts don't get it straight all the time. Announcers and fans alike are occasionally overheard reciting the infield fly parameters. And there is a lot more to the discussion, such as when there is an infield "line drive" situation. But let's keep it clean, shall we? You can pull out the official rulebook for the tawdry details.

In May, 2006, San Francisco's Barry Bonds came up to bat with one out and a runner on first. When he popped up to Dodgers' second baseman Jeff Kent, Bonds started heading back to the dugout, thinking he was automatically out under the infield fly rule. But Kent, a former nemesis, er, teammate of Bonds, dropped the ball. He quickly picked it up and threw to the shortstop, who was covering second base for the force coming from first, and the shortstop threw to first base to get the slacking Bonds. However, Bonds, a fast runner, had already pulled himself together and sprinted to first, narrowly missing being thrown out for the double play. Although he reached first base safely, Bonds was not credited with a hit because Kent could have chosen to throw him out. Instead, Kent threw out the poor chap who was stuck running to second. This is called a "fielder's choice." It means that the fielder decides which guy he wants to get out, often going for the easier of the options. Kent likely could have made the play at first, getting Bonds out, but getting the out at second was a no-brainer. Out of the seven different ways a batter can get on base, the "fielder's choice" is the fourth.

After arriving at first safely, Bonds, a well-seasoned veteran of the game, was overheard getting clarification on what constitutes an infield fly "situation." Barry, Barry, Barry. Grab some paper and a crayon. Okay, runners on first and second . . .

I like baseball because it mimics the rhythms of life: Going away from home, making the journey, then trying like the dickens to come back home again, with plenty of stories to tell.

—Jennifer, 48

CHAPTER 22

Enquiring Mitts Want to Know

Some infield combinations are known for defensive prowess. Other infields operate like sieves. What makes the difference? There are some secrets as to how infielders work together. Much of the necessary teamwork has to do with keeping focused, knowing what the count is, and having a plan of action should the ball come your way. Then there are those teams that act like old married couples. Just as the 1950s sitcom world had the strangely chaste marriage between Lucy and Ricky Ricardo, and today's reality TV world has the strangely indifferent marriages of the "Real Housewives of New York City," the baseball world will always have the enchanted memory of Tinker to Evers to Chance. Huh? Pass the popcorn.

While the prospect of a threesome may have made Lucy blush, this trio of infielders would have excited Ricky, who off-screen was a big baseball fan. Shortstop (6) Joe Tinker, second baseman (4) Johnny Evers and first baseman (3) Frank Chance together made the most famous 6-4-3 double play combination in baseball history while playing for the Chicago Cubs

at the beginning of the twentieth century. In 1910 a *New York Evening Magazine* columnist, Franklin Pierce Adams, memorialized the fielders in his poem "Baseball's Sad Lexicon," written from the point of view of a New York Giants fan:

These are the saddest of possible words:

> *"Tinker to Evers to Chance."*
> *Trio of bear cubs, and fleeter than birds,*
> *Tinker and Evers and Chance.*
> *Ruthlessly pricking our gonfalon bubble,*
> *Making a Giant hit into a double—*
> *Words that are heavy with nothing but trouble:*
> *"Tinker to Evers to Chance."*

While Tinker, Evers, and Chance were all good players, many similarly talented position players, before and since, have gone without a call from Cooperstown. The cohesiveness and adeptness they displayed as a unit ultimately led to their 1946 induction into the Hall of Fame. Their inductions required a vote of the Veterans Committee which, as a reminder, can induct baseball figures that it deems were overlooked. Some say it was Adams' poem that immortalized their names and kept them in the public eye long after they had retired.

We might mention that the third baseman who rounded out the "Tinker to Evers to Chance" infield for five years beginning in 1906 was Harry Steinfeldt, an unexceptional fielder. He was snubbed by the Hall of Fame, maybe because his name didn't easily lend itself to verse. Why should you care? You really shouldn't, but the topic may come up at a cocktail party.

Less famous, but equally fearsome, was the Los Angeles infield from 1973 to 1981. For those eight years Los Angeles Dodgers' fans were treated to what remains the longest-tenured infield team in the history of baseball. It featured Steve Garvey, Davey Lopes, Ron Cey, and Bill Russell. (Pop quiz: they are in order of their position numbers, starting with first base.) The extended honeymoon started when Cey and Lopes were rookies and ended with a bang when Los Angeles beat the Yankees in the 1981 World Series. During the off season, Lopes was traded to Oakland and replaced at second by newbie Steve Sax, who went on to be the fourth consecutive Dodger to win the Rookie of the Year award.

In an age when individual players are unlikely to stay with a single team their whole careers, much less a group of players, it shows how much of a novelty it was to have an entire infield together for so many years. Whether the infield longevity made the Dodgers a better team is up for discussion. And, though they were all voted to the All-Star team, there isn't a Hall of Famer in the lot. Guess they needed a little ditty.

My favorite memory of baseball is my first game. I was about ten and my dad took my sister and me to see the Mariners play the Brewers. I was so excited to go to my first game, but my dad was thrilled. He grew up poor and this was his first game, too. He was more excited than we were.

—Erica, 26

CHAPTER 23

Bats in the Outfield

*I*f you think that the pastoral outfield is where all the ripped, big-hitting, less-acrobatic players go, you are very close. Like anyone on the team, these guys have to parcel out how they spend their practice time. And most of these guys parcel it out in the weight room and batting cage. The focus on brawn often translates into strong arms. And strong arms often make strong throwing arms. That's just what a team needs in the outfield.

But those strong arms don't always do the trick. When a ball is hit to the outfield, a couple of things could happen: the ball is either caught or not caught. It seems simple, but runners complicate matters considerably. Even the best fielders usually cannot throw the ball all the way to a base to get a runner out. Those who can throw with quickness often don't have the pin-point accuracy to get the out, while others may have the accuracy but not the velocity.

Because of the tradeoff between throwing strength and precision, fielders are taught to use the "cutoff man" on a long throw from the outfield. The cutoff man helps keep the opposition's running game at bay by having the outfielder relay the throw through him—usually the second baseman or shortstop—who, in turn, makes the throw to the infield. While some

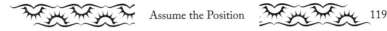 

fielders are capable of making the long throw, many still opt to hit the cutoff. Then there are those fielders who ignore baseball fundamentals and go for the throw. And, sometimes, it's the right choice.

In Game Seven of the 2006 National League pennant series, Mets leftfielder Endy Chavez reached over the outfield fence to steal a two-run homer from Cardinal Scott Rolen. His catch amounted to a great out. However, Chavez wasn't finished; not only did he catch Rolen's ball for one out, he also turned around and assisted in a spectacular and unusual 7-6-3 double play. This is after Chavez noticed that the baserunner, starting from first, had rounded second before discovering that the ball was miraculously caught. In a heads-up play, Chavez threw a bullet to shortstop Jose Reyes (6), whose throw, in turn, got to first baseman (3) Carlos Delgado before the unfortunate baserunner made it back to the sack. These two short, fast throws made the second out a possibility. Not even the best arm from deep left field could have made the long throw to first base so quickly and accurately.

All of that sounds terribly exciting, yes? Well yes, and no. Watching the outfielders on a nice summer day can sometimes be like waiting for a light bulb to burn out. After all, much of a fielder's time is spent routinely jogging around to back up plays that other fielders are supposed to handle. How do the outfielders *not* start daydreaming? Just imagine, it is the middle of a lazy game, and the batter is fouling off pitch after pitch into the stands. The sun is warm against your back and nobody's hit anything your way for two innings. And what about those bitchin' shades you are sporting? No one would notice if you closed your eyes for just a second. Go ahead, we won't tell. Ahhh . . . doesn't that feel good? The murmur of the crowd, the smell of cotton candy, the crack of the bat. Oops—heads up! You may leave with a home-run ball yet.

So outfielders can't just stand out there grazing in the grass, kicking at bugs and soaking up the sunshine. They need to pay attention, especially when there are runners on base. In fact, the fielder has to know where to throw the ball even before it comes to him so he will have the best chance to make a quick throw that results in an out. See, a clever runner may test a fielder's arm the way he would test a catcher's arm while trying to steal a base. In the case of an outfielder, however, a runner may try to stretch a base hit into a double. This can happen when the fielder is known to have a weak throwing arm and is unlikely to get the ball to second base in time to

get the out. But sometimes the fielder surprises the cocky runner by making the difficult throw to second. Whichever play it is, it will likely be a tight play at second.

A similar test occurs when a baserunner opts to head to the next base after a long fly ball is caught. While baserunners may freely run on a hit to the outfield, they must wait on a fly ball. They are waiting for the ball to be caught so they can tag up and try to run to the next base. This is the same tagging scenario that plays out when a batter hits a sacrifice fly, an offensive tactic discussed in Chapter 17, "Sacrifice." Anyway, back to the game. A fly ball is hit. The fans wait. The runner waits. The ball flies up, up, up. The runner eyes the fielder, sizing up the competition . . . can he make it to the next base safely? Sure, he's fast. But the other guy's got a good arm. Then, the ball drops into the fielder's glove. How might this scene pan out?

Sheesh. A better question is why all the drama? Well, it's because of the rule that states when a batted ball is caught, the baserunner must return to his base and "tag up" before proceeding onward. The tension builds when, on a high fly ball to the outfield—one that will certainly be caught—the runner digs in on his base, like a sprinter on the blocks, preparing to run as soon as the ball is caught. Or maybe the runner just wants the fielder to think he is going to run. You know, give the outfielder a little something extra to think about while he tries to make the catch. If the runner chooses to stay put on that long fly ball—or not try to stretch a single into a double, as mentioned above—the fielder "held" the runner on base. Ultimately, it is a sign of respect from the runner, a nod to a strong arm.

But if the runner decides to go, the outfielder may try to beat him to the next base with a mighty throw, and the play will result in either an assist from the outfielder or the runner reaching base safely. One way or the other, this is an exciting play to watch, particularly when the runner in question is on third base and the outfielder is trying to make the throw to home to prevent that runner from scoring. You may see lots of guys running when a rookie outfielder is playing, in an effort to take advantage of the rookie's inexperience or just to see what he's made of.

Previously, you read about Endy Chavez's heads-up double play during the 2006 playoffs. The first out was a spectacular catch. The second out was because the Cardinals' Jim Edmonds didn't tag up. An experienced baserunner, Edmonds was on first base when the ball was hit deep to left field. He started running, thinking that the ball was surely headed over the fence,

which it was. Everyone saw that. Chavez just brought it back. When the fly ball was caught, Edmonds was nowhere near tagging up on first base. Rather, he was heading for third. When he saw that Chavez had the ball, Edmonds tried to return to first base but was thrown out for the double play. Find the replay. It was a remarkable play.

The outfielder lined up on the third-base side of the outfield is the left fielder (7), or position number seven. Left fielders are commonly thought of as a pretty useless defensive bunch, in general, and are assigned to the position because the rules dictate that someone needs to stand there. Lonnie Smith quilted together a seventeen-year career with various teams that spanned the reign of disco, in the late 1970s, to grunge, in the early 1990s. Smith's non-existent fielding earned him the nickname "Skates" because he often fell while going for a ball or going to recover a ball that he had dropped. Those replays could be worth looking at, too.

But that anecdote—and many, many others—doesn't mean that all left fielders are wretched. Many have been trusty fielders. Ted Williams, though he often appeared a bit bored with the whole fielding thing, was a solid defender for the Red Sox. And Stan "The Man" Musial is known as one of the best left fielders in the game, even though he only played a third of his games at that position. See, it doesn't take much to be considered a great left fielder. But Williams and "The Man" are best known for their hitting.

It is rare that a left fielder will win a Gold Glove because there is normally a supremely more talented guy in center field who runs faster, jumps higher, and throws farther. Left fielders don't need a great arm because they aren't often responsible for making the long throws that are required from center field or right field. If they were that good, they'd be playing one of those other positions.

But the glitz doesn't always go to the center fielder. Minnie Minoso (not Mendoza!) played for several teams and won three Gold Gloves at left field. Carl Yastrzemski got seven when he played for the Boston Red Sox from 1961 to 1983. And Barry Bonds earned eight through 2007. But these three are an anomaly, and that's not just because Bonds' home-run output had curiously increased with age. Nor is it because of Minnie's bizarre comeback with the White Sox at age fifty-four. This publicity stunt in 1980 made him the only player with major league at bats in five decades. Please note that we didn't say he got a hit in five decades, just that he got up to bat.

Center field (8) is the glory position in the outfield. The number-eight-position player completes the strong middle that a team strives for, beginning with the catcher and including the shortstop and second baseman. A team leader on the field, the center fielder coordinates the play to ensure there isn't a collision when two fielders go for the same ball. There is a lot of real estate to cover in center field, and it needs to be covered with fast legs and a strong arm. Because of these dual talents, center fielders are also known for being speedy around the bases and talented hitters, or at least the really good ones are.

Willie Mays' speed, athleticism, and longevity in the center field spot put him in the running to be considered one of the best players in the history of the game. He had all the five "tools" on which a player is judged: running, catching, throwing, hitting, and hitting for power. Mays was not only a contact hitter who got on base, he was also capable of hitting the ball really hard. This is a rare and valuable combination for a hitter because it makes him a unpredictable at the plate—in a way that unsettles pitchers. The Hall of Famer started his career winning the Rookie of the Year award in 1951 while playing for the New York Giants and continued to wow crowds throughout his career with his powerful strokes of the bat, which garnered him extra base hits and home runs. In the following years, Mays wowed the fans with diving defensive plays, bare-handed catches, and spectacular throws to catch runners who foolishly thought they could safely make it to the next base. During his twenty-two-year career, he made 195 such assists and won twelve consecutive Gold Gloves. He likely would have earned more, but the award wasn't offered for the first six years of his career.

Mays' speed and overall hustle made possible his record of 7,095 catches, or "putouts," from his outfield post, surpassing that of Richie Ashburn by 1,000. Another outstanding fielder, Ashburn played seven seasons fewer than Mays, which, when taken into consideration, makes his fielding statistics more aligned with those of Mays. On the batting side, however, Ashburn was a typical contact hitter. He was consistently among those players leading the league in hits, yet tallied only twenty-nine homers during his career. No slouch, Mays also had many hits. It's just that 660 of them went over the fence, and Endy Chavez wasn't there to bring them back.

The Dodgers' Andruw Jones and Cincinnati's Ken Griffey, Jr., are both five-tool center fielders who are working out to have parallel careers, on

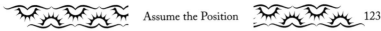

paper. Nearing the end of his career at center field, Griffey is closing in on 600 home runs and his defensive production won ten consecutive Gold Gloves, beginning in 1990, his second season. Similarly, Jones has ten consecutive Gold Gloves in his twelve seasons, almost 400 dingers, and enough of an arm to make smart speedsters think twice before taking another step.

The final position player is the right fielder (9), or the number-nine guy. This is the spot where certain little league players are sent to cause the least amount of trouble for their team. As we indicated before, the lame duck position in the majors falls to the other "corner," the left field. Somewhere between fifth grade and college, the right-field position morphs into something relatively important. Still, its level of importance hinges on who is occupying the space. Take Babe Herman, for example. Herman was a fierce batter who averaged .324 over his thirteen-year career, which started with the Dodgers in 1926. He nearly hit .400 in 1930, but he was an atrocious right fielder. A teammate once said that he wore a glove only "because it was league custom."

The Seattle Mariners' Ichiro Suzuki is considered among the best to have played right field. Drafted in 2001 out of the Japanese major leagues, he won both the Rookie of the Year and Most Valuable Player awards in the same year, an honor that had happened only once before—in 1975 with Boston's Fred Lynn, then a twenty-three-year-old center fielder. Ichiro's slap-hitting style, much like Ashburn's, has helped him lead the league in several batting categories. As with any good outfielder, Ichiro's speed is important to covering his turf. Additionally, he's earned the Gold Glove every year through 2007, amassed 2,546 putouts, and contributed sixty six assists. Many of these same qualities helped in the decision to move him to center field in the middle of the 2006 season. That, and the fact that the Mariners were in desperate need of a center fielder.

In 1960, twenty-five-year-old Roberto Clemente helped lead his Pittsburgh Pirates to the franchise's first World Series championship in thirty-five years. While he performed well at the plate during the series, it was his fielding that started to grab the attention of fans and players. In Game Four, after Yankee Bill "Moose" Skowron jacked a home run over Clemente's head in the forth inning, he tried it again in the seventh; this time, though, the ball bounced in bounds before going over the outfield fence. Because the ball went out of play, it was ruled a "ground-rule double,"

which means Skowron got to take second base. With the Yankees trailing, 1-3, and Skowron in scoring position, Gil McDougald stepped up to the plate and nailed a single to deep right field. Clemente fielded the ball and fired a rocket directly to his catcher in an effort to throw Skowron out at home. But Skowron had stopped at third. Smart. It's also worth noting that Clemente did not follow sound baseball fundamentals by using the cutoff man. But he's Roberto Clemente. He's in the Hall of Fame.

I listened to Atlanta Braves (when they were really bad) games on the radio growing up because I wasn't allowed to read in bed after lights out! I remember hearing the radio call of Hank Aaron's record-breaking 715th home run in bed at night . . . That was pretty cool!

—Brita, 44

CHAPTER 24

Utility

*E*very major league club has utility players. They are the Lenny Harrises, Bob Kennedys, Jose Oquendoses, and Ryan Freelses of the world. Don't know who these guys are? Exactly. They are baseball's jacks-of-all-trades. These backup players are guys who can play a number of positions on the field. They are called upon to replace starting players when the starter is injured, sick, or in need of a break. Every team needs a fleet of reliable backup players. It gives a team depth.

While in the minor leagues, a player may learn a number of different positions to make himself more attractive to major league coaches. Yankees catcher Jorge Posada did that. He came up through the minor leagues as a second baseman but was told that he had a better shot at making the majors as a catcher. So he switched positions and eventually landed a role as New York's starting catcher. Many others aren't so lucky. When they make it to the majors these guys rarely get promoted to a coveted regular spot on a major league team. Instead, they become utility players, regularly assigned to different positions and playing infrequently. This isn't ideal, of course, but we're not feeling too sorry for them. There are some people who actually work in an office all day.

There are many major league starters who have played more than one position, but they are not considered utility players. For instance, during his twenty-four-year career Pete Rose played every position except shortstop and catcher; Hall of Famer Ernie Banks was both a star shortstop and a star first baseman. Gil McDougald started at third, second, and shortstop throughout his ten-year career. Even though they played lots of positions, these three guys were talented superstars, not utility players waiting for their big break and a chance to be a team fixture. They owned several starting jobs; most utility players don't get even one.

Utility player Rich Aurilia was once the Giant's starter at shortstop but, by the time he landed in Cincinnati in 2005—before heading back to San Francisco in 2007—he was a bona fide utility guy. And he had a refreshingly good-natured, blue-collar attitude to go with his new, less-glamorous role. "We'll see where Waldo is tomorrow," he told *The Cincinnati Enquirer* in 2006, referring to his elusive role on the team. "I come in and see if my name's in the lineup. Then I check the little box to the right to see where I'm playing," he added.

Lenny Harris played for several National League teams during his eighteen-year career, beginning in 1988 with Cincinnati. He played every position but catcher and never won an award or starting position. This includes a brief pitching stint in 1998 that lasted one successful inning. His determination and affable clubhouse demeanor paid off when he won one of those gaudy World Series Championship rings while playing with the Florida Marlins in 2003. Bling aside, Harris' work proved lucrative, too, earning him more than $11 million over the course of his career. Not starting wages, mind you, but a decent living nonetheless.

Speaking of money, Phil Linz was a career backup player while with the Yankees for most of his seven seasons during mid-1960s. Linz played shortstop, second base, third base, and a little outfield. For this adaptable spirit, he was handsomely rewarded—earning an annual salary of about $20,000 by his mid-career. And his supplementary status seemed to amuse him. He was once quoted as saying: "You can't get rich sitting on the bench, but I'm giving it a try."

Not everyone is as happy about their position as a non-starter. Veteran Tony Womack spent much of the 2005 season fighting for the Yankees' starting second-baseman job only to lose it to rookie Robinson Cano. During the season Womack ended up playing four positions. In December

of that year he was traded to Cincinnati for two minor league players and a little cash. Not quite as bad as being traded for a camel and a box of Froot Loops, as Jose Canseco regarded one of his trades, but it's probably not what the 1997 All-Star had pictured for his professional baseball career, even if it was in its twilight.

> *Baseball is like a chess game played on a bigger gameboard with greater strategy and out in the great outdoors.*
>
> —*Sherry, 52*

He Never Saw the Error of his Ways

There are other stats to turn to, but few are more discussed than the one that charts a fielder's mistakes. Maybe it is because we can all relate to missing a diving catch or to misfiring a throw that ends up going four feet over the first baseman's head. That's if we could even throw it that far. These are all things we spectators understand.

As impressive as a good defensive move can look, some moves just don't work out; even the easy ones sometimes get away. When that happens, the fielder is pegged with an "error," a defensive statistic of which no one wants to lead the league. An error is given to a fielder when he tries and fails to make the play that he is supposed to make. A simple example is when an outfielder drops a lazy fly ball. Major leaguers get paid to make that catch. And we pay to see them make it. When a batter reaches base because of a fielder's error, he doesn't get credit for a hit. It is, essentially, a mistake that he is on base at all. Did we say he got on base?! Holy backstop, Batboy! This makes an "error," the fifth way a batter can

reach base safely. So, of the seven ways to get on base, we've covered five: the error, the hit, the walk, the fielder's choice, and, possibly the grittiest of all, being hit by a pitch.

As most of us have only watched from the sidelines, it is often difficult to judge whether a play should have been made. Well, spectator or not, you aren't alone. As with everything about this game, there are often debates among experts as to whether a player should be given an error on any given play. Is the player expected to catch the lazy fly ball with the sun in his eyes? A screaming line drive gets past the diving shortstop? A rock in the infield makes the ball hop up and the fielder can't field it cleanly? How about when the second baseman is trying to turn a double play and the runner, who by this point is out at second, forces the fielder to jump up in the air and make the throw to first from an angle that defies the laws of gravity? Circumstances such as these can make it difficult to determine whether a play is an error or not. The final judgment as to how a play should be scored—maybe a hit, maybe an error—falls on the shoulders of the official scorer. Each team employs an MLB-approved scorer to cover its home games. These scoring decisions are often considered controversial because they affect players' batting averages and many other statistics.

During a May 5, 1917, game between the St. Louis Browns and the Chicago White Sox, scorer J. B. Sheridan agonized over how Chicago's Buck Weaver got on base in the first inning. There was some debate that Weaver got on base because of an error by the second baseman, who was unable to make the throw to first baseman George Sisler in time for the out. But Sheriden gave Weaver the hit. However, it is possible that the scorer began to question that decision with every passing inning. This is because Ernie Koob, the Brown's pitcher, didn't allow another hit for the rest of the game. Thus, the disputable scoring decision in the first inning—which gave Weaver a hit—effectively robbed Koob of one of the ultimate pitching triumphs: the no-hitter. This prompted Sheridan to question players, umpires and coaches at the end of the game about how they saw the first-inning play. With new information, Sheridan took away Weaver's hit and, instead, tagged the second baseman with an error; Koob got his no-hitter. However, the decision took so long that Chicago and St. Louis newspapers were printed with different results—one reporting Koob's one-hitter and the other announcing the no-hitter. The Browns won the game, 1-0.

Major league records for consecutive errorless games at any given position are a benchmark to which outstanding fielders strive. While playing for the Oakland A's and San Francisco Giants in the early 1990s, outfielder and Gold Glove winner Darren Lewis secured a place in the record books by amassing 369 consecutive errorless major league games. The speed that helped him cover his territory in the field paid off for him as a hitter and at the bank: he was the league leader in triples in 1994, and the Giants paid him five times his salary the following year.

Errors are often embarrassing, but not many are as humiliating as Jose Canseco's blunder in 1993 while playing for the Texas Rangers. Instead of making the out that he was expected to make, he accomplished the polar opposite: giving the opposing team a home run. On May 26, Canseco jumped up by the outfield wall to catch Carlos Martinez's long fly ball. It would have been a tremendous catch, but instead it became a tremendous blooper highlight. Canseco miscalculated the trajectory of the ball, which bounced off his head and over the outfield fence, giving the Indians a home run.

Few errors are as replayed on TV and in nightmares as Bill Buckner's blunder during Game Six of the 1986 World Series. All the Red Sox first baseman had to do to win Boston its first Championship in sixty-eight years was field a slow grounder that Mookie Wilson hit and step on the base for the final out of the series. Instead, the ball rolled slowly between the veteran's legs and out into shallow right field. This error allowed Wilson to get on base and, more importantly, Ray Knight to score the winning run from second base. This error led to the following day's Game Seven in New York, which the Mets won, forever linking Buckner with the team's eighty-nine-year championship drought, which was eventually snapped in 2004.

I think every Boston fan remembers where they were during the series in which the ball rolled through Bill Buckner's legs. The next night, in the final game against the Mets, we were one strike away from winning the World Series. I was at my cousin's house. We were beside ourselves with excitement and tension. My cousin says to me, "They could lose it all right now with one wild pitch." And what happens? Right at that moment, the Red Sox pitcher delivers a wild pitch. The Mets advanced. The rest is history. My cousin fell onto the floor in front of the TV and was beating the floor with his fists!

—Lisa, 49

SECTION FIVE

A School Boy's
Perfect Profession

To grow up and make a living doing nothing but throwing things looks like Utopia to most ten-year-old boys; to think that some grown up men get to live out that fantasy, getting gobs of money for the pain and pleasure, seems just wrong. But, there it is. And here we are, in this section, where we'll give lots of space to pitchers, otherwise regarded as the delicate *prima donnas* of the team.

We all know that baseball games are won not only by scoring runs but also by preventing the other team from accumulating any, and the first line of defense for preventing this is pitching. Because of this, teams are always looking to build a crack pitching staff. After all, good pitchers are supposed to keep hitters—even the best ones—from getting on base. But it just so happens that there is a dearth of pitchers dominant enough to sway the outcome of games on a regular basis. This is why you might hear that certain teams are in need of a true starting pitcher, otherwise known as the team's "ace." Or maybe the managers are hoping to add to the roster a commanding closer, one who specializes in finishing games.

But really, as much as anything else, we dedicate a chapter to pitchers because, as a group, they make for really entertaining reading. They can be quirky, mischievous, and somewhat paranoid; the poor guys would just be bored silly in the outfield. That's why the league keeps most of them cooped up in the bullpen, where they are free to misbehave.

## CHAPTER 26

Is That a Can of Pine Tar in Your Pocket or Are You Just Happy to See Me?

All the attention being showered on pitchers these days is in stark contrast to how pitchers were initially perceived. In the 1850s, for instance, the pitcher was often regarded among the least important and least athletic players on the field. Their role was to toss the ball gingerly up so the batter could hit it really hard. Bonus points if it was a home run! To emasculate them even further, pitchers were required to throw the ball underhand. And this was not underhand as you see in fast-pitch softball, where the pitcher's arm frighteningly whirls around like the spokes on a wagon wheel as the carriage careens into a prairie ravine. No. It is "underhand" like Great Aunt

Julia throwing horseshoes at the summer barbeque with one hand while holding a gin and tonic with her other.

This role didn't last terribly long as pitchers grew increasingly frustrated with their lame status, wanting to get credit for more outs and to be defensive contributors. So they started pushing the limits of the rules. Looking for an edge, pitchers experimented with jerky deliveries, wild windups, and a slightly "sideways" release rather than the league-mandated underhand pitch. This initiated an era of more exciting, harder-to-hit pitches—a fastball with a little zing for example. Spurred by his comrades, Candy Cummings mastered the curveball, a new pitch that quickly became synonymous with pitcher success and batter distress. Before long, league owners had no choice but to remove any restrictions on how pitchers could throw the ball. While a seemingly charitable salvo, this concession was just a carrot. But you know what came next? Yep, the stick.

In 1887 the league invented the strike zone and required pitchers to deliver the ball within this imaginary rectangle above home plate. It was intended to tip the balance of power that pitchers had grown accustomed to by way of the mighty curveball back into the hitter's corner. The contrived nature of this latest rule left the growing number of skilled pitchers befuddled but undeterred.

For their part, pitchers already knew they had become important in the eyes of baseball when their performance was charted by a new brand of statistics. Fans and sportswriters started keeping track of everything from how many strikeouts a pitcher threw to how many runs the other team scored off a pitcher. For better or worse, it became clear that pitchers had an influence on the outcome of games. Unofficially, pitchers started to get credit for a "win" when they participated in a winning game.

By the end of July, 1890, the Cleveland Spiders, owned by the Robison brothers, were in the middle of an atrocious year, having lost twenty-five of their last thirty-one games. Looking for a boost, the team picked up Cy Young, a relatively unknown pitcher, from a team in nearby Canton for $500. Young allowed three singles and went on to win his inaugural major league game against Cap Anson and his Chicago Cubs, 8-1. A buzz soon swirled around Young and his tireless arm. The next year, his twenty-seven wins accounted for 42 percent of the team's victories. By the time Young retired after twenty-two seasons he had 511 wins under his belt, a major league record rivaled only by Walter Johnson, who won 417 games

throughout twenty-one years pitching for the Washington Senators in the early 1900s. While both Hall of Famers are considered among the best ever to play the game, it was Young's career that was recognized in 1956 when Commissioner Ford Frick created the Cy Young award to honor each year's most valuable pitcher. As mentioned in Chapter Eight, "Branching Out," Don Newcombe, one of the game's early black superstars, was the award's first recipient. He also snagged the National League's Most Valuable Player that same year. This recognition is all the more noteworthy considering the racial strife that existed at the time in baseball and throughout the country. In 1956, three MLB teams had yet to integrate. Additionally, in 1949 Newcombe won the Rookie of the Year award, making him the only player to have earned all three awards.

Around the same time that Young made his debut in 1890, rules makers thought they'd seen enough. Pitching had run amok and the hitting game was reduced to pieces. Fans wanted to see big hits and started to turn away. There was little hope for this dilemma until the league adopted a suggestion by Philadelphia sportswriter W.R. Lester that required pitchers to throw from farther back from home plate. Conceivably this would give batters more time to react to a pitch and the hitting game would once again become king.

It worked. Pitchers in 1894 struggled to adapt to this new setup. Many failed terribly. As a group, they allowed more runners on base as compared to previous years, and home runs spiked. Even Cy Young's stats nosedived. It took a while to adjust to the longer distance, but pitchers were resolute. They spent the next two decades swapping strategy, sandpaper, and secrets, determined to regain prominence by whatever means necessary.

Their opening gambit was to "doctor" the ball covertly. This was achieved in a number of ways. Pitchers would grease the ball because slick substances helped create an unpredictable path to the plate, making the ball more difficult for batters to track and hit. Batters had difficulty seeing a ball barreling toward them if it was camouflaged with aptly applied dirt, licorice, or tobacco juice. And if they can't see it, they can't hit it! Pitchers experimented with nicking the ball with their fingernails, sandpaper, rocks, and, even better, a nail file concealed in the glove. A surgically-applied cut on one spot of the ball enhanced the spin of a pitch and made for some truly knee-buckling curveballs. Pitchers discovered that a schmear of pine tar helped them grip the ball better, making for faster throws. Then there came

the slimy and unpredictable spitball. Soon, other less slithery pitches were in vogue: the forkball, the screwball, and the knuckleball.

Flush with success, pitchers continued to roll. During that same time-frame, they had also became chummy with the groundskeepers at the home stadium and enlisted their help in a plot to take over the world. Soon, pitchers had designer mounds from which to hurl. The height of the mounds gave them leverage that neutralized the longer distance from which they now had to throw.

Nothing about this, er, creativity was exactly considered corrupt. But the free-rolling life wasn't to last—on or off the field. During these years that the baseball world tussled with its demons, the rest of the country was working up to see the day when the FBI was called in to conduct raids on illegal gin joints, and women were granted the right to vote. Perhaps, sensing this social upheaval, baseball owners no longer wanted to sit idly by and allow pitchers to continue on in their somewhat lawless fashion. In order to restore balance to the game, the league outlawed some forms of doctored balls, starting in 1915 with the scuffed up "emery" ball, a wily pitch created by scuffing the surface of the ball with an emery board. Then the league set limits on the height of mounds, a standard that was anything but standard for the next several decades. But pitchers continued to dominate.

That is, until early evening in New York's Polo Grounds on August 16, 1920. On that day, Ray Chapman, the Cleveland Indians' beloved twenty-nine-year-old shortstop, was hit in the head by a pitch from Yankee Carl Mays, a fastballer with an underhand, or "submarine," delivery. Chapman died the following morning, leaving behind his new wife, Katie, and unborn daughter.

The outrage was visceral. Within days, teams threatened to boycott games in which Mays pitched. Then, a week later, as Mays was set to pitch against the Detroit Tigers, his first game since the tragedy, he became rattled when he was handed a note from Detroit's Ty Cobb. It read, "If it was within my power, I would have inscribed on Ray Chapman's tombstone these words: 'Here lies a victim of arrogance, viciousness, and greed.'"

As you can imagine, there was a lot of hearsay and emotion surrounding the event. This makes it all the more important to stump for Mays and point out some of the factors that suggest that maybe he wasn't as barbaric as many liked to believe. First, it is true that the day's wet field could have contributed to a slippery ball and an ensuing feral pitch. Second, as the

overcast day progressed, Chapman and other batters probably had a hard time seeing the ball, which, since umpires rarely replaced game balls during that era, was likely very dirty. And, third, Chapman was among the many batters who stood close to the plate to get a better look at the incoming pitch. This strategy is still cited as a reason why some batters are hit by pitches. But there was no amount of justification or rationalization or stumping that would spare Mays a lifetime of defensiveness. He constantly denied accusations that he irresponsibly lost control of a spitball, a tricky pitch that baseball ruled illegal early in 1920. Worse were the charges that he purposefully "beaned" Chapman. It didn't help Mays' case that he was going for his 100th career win that night. Was he more aggressive than normal with that significant benchmark in reach? Yes or no, he lost the game in which Chapman was hit, but reached his 100th win in his next start, the game against Cobb's Tigers.

And what's a sad story without an equally moving epilogue? For starters, Stanley Coveleski, Cleveland's starting pitcher that fateful night, had a career that closely paralleled Mays'. In 1969, the Veterans Committee had kind words for the spitballer and inducted Coveleski into the Hall of Fame. But Mays died two years later without the call from Cooperstown, and the Chapman tragedy is often cited as the reason why. Another Hall of Famer, Joe Sewell, was the stocky rookie tapped to fill Cleveland's tragically vacant shortstop position. Two months after Chapman's death, his Indians rallied to win the first of the franchise's two World Series titles. But making the story even more punishing is that Chapman's wife and daughter were dead seven years later, the former by suicide, the latter by measles.

The Chapman tragedy was the final blow to the "dead-ball era," a period starting in the early 1900s and marked by various factors that stoked pitchers' dominance. For one, the incident forced owners to adhere to an existing rule banning overused balls. No longer did team lackeys scurry into the stands to retrieve dingy foul balls in order to cycle them back into play. And because any substance applied to a ball would discolor it and make it more difficult for batters to see, Chapman's death led to the end of all doctored balls. Unfortunately it didn't lead to batting helmets, which likely would have saved Chapman. This equipment was not mandatory until more than fifty years later.

We mentioned Chapman's death led to the end of all doctored balls. Well, let us clarify: the incident led to end of the *legal* use of doctored balls.

Yes, pay attention, and you will see that many outlawed pitches and ploys are still pretty common in the pitcher's arsenal, which also includes legitimate pitches such as the fastball and the curveball. In the 1970s Dodger Don Sutton was nicknamed "Black & Decker" because of the tools that he used to doctor the ball, such as his wedding ring, his filed-down belt buckle, or a sheet of sandpaper. And Detroit's Kenny Rogers was accused of doctoring the ball with pine tar during his stint on the mound in Game Two of the 2006 World Series. Rogers claimed that the yellowish stain on his palm was dirt. Doesn't everyone know that Rogers likes to relax by spending time in his cherished flower garden before big games? Boys will be boys. It's just that it's not so cute when the "boys" are forty-one-year-old cheaters.

We're not sure why this is, but all ballplayers seem inclined to cheat. So why get in a huff about a little trickery from the mound? Certainly hitters flirt with the game's boundaries, sometimes crafting bats to accommodate their hitting styles. Others may cheat by stuffing hollowed-out bats with superballs or cork to help the baseball ricochet off the bat—for extra bases—when it makes contact with a pitch. However, pitchers seem particularly predisposed to their brand of cunning. The trait is deliciously woven into the cloth of the position, harkening back to the early days when a pitcher had to fight—or cheat—for the right to compete. But maybe that's just the romantic in us talking. Until recently, getting caught cheating on the mound was often considered a badge of honor, punished only with a knowing glance and wonkish mutterings. Now it's punishable by a ten-game suspension. So much for rose petals on our pillows.

A level of graciousness is supposed to accompany the deviousness. But some pitchers still regard the ability to doctor the ball as a trick of the trade, scoffing at the idea that they won't do something just because a pesky thing called the rulebook instructs them not to. The Hall of Fame's Gaylord Perry pitched for twenty-two years starting in the early 1960s and was brazen about his use of illegal pitches. In 2006, Perry told a reporter that the day before he was to pitch, he would approach the opposing team while they were warming up for the game and, with his hand slathered in Vaseline, shake their hands. When the grossed-out players rightfully demanded an explanation, the smirking farm boy would reply that he was, "Gettin' ready for tomorrow night's game."

With doctored balls outlawed in 1920, pitchers simply became more creative. The knuckleball, an erratic and often impossible pitch to hit, became

quite popular. Hoyt Wilhelm thought the knuckleball was an ingenious invention. After earning a Purple Heart in World War II, the Hall of Famer broke into the majors at the age of twenty-nine and lasted another two decades on the mound, retiring in the middle of the 1972 season. This longevity—and that of just about any knuckleballer—stems from the fact that the knuckleball is inherently easy on the arm. It also reduces the need to practice an array of pitches. "You don't need variations," Wilhelm said of the knuckleball. "The damn ball jumps around so crazily, it's like having 100 pitches."

There are two kinds of pitchers in the baseball world working today: those who throw fastballs and those who throw "junk." A fastballer might throw at a speed upwards of 100 miles per hour, hopefully over the plate. He tries to intimidate batters with sheer brawn and velocity. Junkballers, on the other hand, focus their time on various "off-speed" pitches, such as the curveball, screwball, and knuckleball, which top out around seventy-five miles per hour. On the surface, it seems like it would be a refreshing break to be dealt an off-speed pitch to wallop. But don't be tricked. These pitches are intended to mess with batters' timing. And just so you don't get too comfy with the whole idea, the timing ploy isn't the exclusive terrain of junkballers. Some of the elite fastball heroes tease their prey by throwing an off-speed curveball only to follow it with a blistering zinger. When a pitcher messes with the batter's mind, er, timing, it's said that he is "setting up the hitter."

Pitcher's note to self: Whenever you have a chance to screw with a batter's groove, do it.

Fans need not look any further than the home run carnival of the late 1990s to see why league honchos have historically tried to keep pitchers from becoming overly dominant. We are nutty for the long ball. The dinger. The home run. And this is no recent phenomenon. The latter part of the 1960s saw an increase in attendance after changes were made to rein in the power of pitchers. And the taste for the tater goes back even farther. When pitchers were saddled with a longer distance to throw from in 1895—a change that led to higher scoring games—attendance went up significantly from only a few years before. In the early 1900s, baseball grew in popularity for many different reasons but, ultimately, pitcher dominance took its toll and resulted in a loss of fans in the stands. In fact, hitting and attendance

continued to spiral downward until 1920, when the game was resuscitated by Babe Ruth's slug parade.

For me there is not one specific baseball memory that is best. In every phase of my life, baseball has been there. As a kid, I have fond memories of watching the Dodgers at my Grammy's house. As I grew up, baseball was a social outlet. My girlfriends and I would spend our summers watching boyfriends' (or wishing they were our boyfriends) summer ball games. As an adult, baseball has given me and friends an outlet for still feeling like a kid.

—*Jen, 37*

Stretching out the Canvas

It hasn't always been easy for pitchers, has it? They've had to fight for their rightful place every step of the way and come up with inventive ways to stay relevant. The scheming worked. The pitching contingent picked a dogfight, won many battles, and ended up shaping the game into what it is today. The flurry of changes in baseball's early years achieved an acceptable balance by 1900, the widely recognized mark for "modern baseball." By this point, the kinks had been worked out and, with few exceptions, the game looked much like it does today. This is also when baseball started having to acknowledge—and deal with—the rivalry between pitchers and hitters. Much like Christmas at the Cleavers, there needed to be balance and fairness. Sure, we love our home runs; but we like to see winning teams, too. It was soon obvious that strong pitching was key to winning games. Pitcher value skyrocketed because winning teams lure fans. Fans buy lots of popcorn. In St. Louis, they bought lots of beer. This was all very important to owners.

In 1878, the Boston Red Caps topped the major leagues with Tommy Bond pitching in fifty-nine of the season's sixty games. He completed fifty-seven of those games and won forty. The team's only backup pitcher was

John Manning, who pitched a mere eleven innings. The team didn't need another pitcher. And, as the team's speedy outfielder and one of Boston's best hitters, Manning was pretty busy with his other job, anyway.

When Boston won its eighth title twenty years later, the league had changed considerably. Not only were there newfangled pitches and rules, the league had doubled the number of teams and more than doubled the number of games. Coupled with the strenuous overhand pitch, which made its debut in the 1880s, the sport had become too taxing for a pitcher to handle the workload solo. For their part, Boston rotated through four starting pitchers in 1898, including Hall of Famers Kid Nichols and Vic Willis. As Boston discovered, pitching became so valued that all teams began stockpiling pitchers, having a few backup guys and as many as six regular pitchers in the rotation. This arrangement enabled managers to start games with a different pitcher until he rotated through all of them. This gave pitchers suitable rest before their next game, or "start."

During that time frame, it also became valuable to have a left-handed pitcher on staff. Among other things, it was theorized that throwing the powerful curveball was more natural for a lefty, and that right-handed hitters—the majority—couldn't see the pitch as well coming from a lefty. It is also theoretically easier for lefty pitchers to "pick off" runners taking a big head start, or "lead," off of first base. Runners can often take a lead without reprisal because they need to be tagged with the ball to be out. And though there have been some trick plays, the ball is usually with the pitcher, too far away to get tagged. So the runner may take a lead off the base to prepare to steal second base or even just to unsettle the pitcher, a worthy goal. Whichever reason, you'll occasionally see the pitcher throw the ball to the first baseman in an effort to get the runner out. This is the pick-off throw. A savvy runner will scurry or dive back to first base before the first baseman can tag him out with the ball. This back-and-forth may happen several times during a single at bat and is an indication that the runner has disrupted the pitcher. Sometimes a pitcher may make this pick-off throw just to keep the runner close to the bag—don't want baserunners getting too confident, you know. But if the runner ventures too far off base, or if he's not paying attention when the pick-off throw comes in, he may be tagged with the ball before he can return to the base. He's out. This is a successful pick off and an embarrassing defeat for the baserunner. Many say that this play is easier for lefties because the lefty pitcher is staring at the runner on

first base before the pitch is thrown; right-handed pitchers have their backs to first base.

A pitcher's worth to a team is in keeping opponents off of the bases. One of the tricks to do this is to throw pitches that blow by batters for strikes. Another way is to deliver tricky pitches that, while more likely to get hit, are also likely to produce relatively easy, garden-variety outs such as a routine ground ball or a lazy pop fly. Keeping runners off the basepaths is the primary responsibility of the pitcher, but, since they cannot throw the ball past the hitter all the time, they rely on the other fielders to chip in for the victory by catching the balls that come their way. Or, more accurately, by running and diving to make the difficult plays.

Pitchers are known to throw occasional no-hitters, which means that batters can still get on base from walks or fielding errors. During Hall of Famer Nolan Ryan's twenty-seven-year career he pitched seven no-hitters—a major league record. He also tacked on twelve one-hitters for good measure.

As you'd expect, Ryan won all of his no-hitters, as most pitchers do, but every once in a while, a pitcher isn't as lucky. You know, if a guy finds his way on base, he is likely to try to score. This is like our hustling pal Pete Rose, who spoiled Ken Johnson's no-hitter party on April 23, 1964, making him the first pitcher to throw such a game and lose. In the top of the ninth inning, and with the score tied, 0-0, Rose got on base through an error by Johnson. Then, Rose went to work, annoying the Houston defense as he scored by way of a stolen base and another fielding error. Since Johnson's team couldn't manage to post any offense in the bottom of the ninth inning, the poor guy ended up losing the only no-hitter of his career, 1-0.

The Holy Grail of the pitching world is delivering the "perfect game." A pitcher throws a perfect game when he completes a game during which no one from the other team ever reaches base. For the mathematically challenged, that's twenty-seven guys up and twenty-seven guys down. Perfect games have been pitched only seventeen times in MLB history and never by the same pitcher twice. This rare feat takes some doing, and not just by the pitcher and fielders. Some think it requires divine intervention.

About eight weeks after Rose single-handedly beat Johnson, Philadelphia's sidearm pitcher Jim Bunning met with some luck in a game against the New York Mets. Having thrown a no-hitter in 1958, the father of seven found himself faced with the possibility of a perfect game

on Father's Day, 1964. Bunning, who was a future Hall of Famer and future U.S. congressman, struck out ten hitters that day but needed help from his fielders for the remaining seventeen outs, and reportedly told them to, "Dive for every one!" Indeed, assistance was required. One such play happened in the fifth inning when Philly's second baseman Tony Taylor grabbed a hard ground ball and, falling to his knees, kept Jesse Gonder off base by making a spectacular throw to first for the out. Bunning's perfect game was in the works.

I love the way when I am at the ballpark watching the game I forget I have a job, a mortgage, and any responsibilities.

—Anonymous

CHAPTER 28

Measuring the Man

*A*s can be seen in the cases of perfect games and no-hitters, pitchers require assistance from the team to make these pursuits possible. Batters need to hit; fielders need to catch. Likewise, giving a starting pitcher the win for contributing to that day's game sometimes overstates his importance. The other team can make big mistakes. And acrobatic fielders play a role, just like those who helped Bunning secure his perfect game. Not to slight pitchers' efforts, mind you. But these guys don't even need to pitch the whole game to get credit for the win! Come on. A starting pitcher who pitches the first five innings and leaves when his team is in the lead—and keeps it—gets the win. Certainly, guys who have a lot of wins during the course of a season should be considered good pitchers; they often put their teams in a good position to win the game. But, despite all the best efforts of all the best pitchers, sometimes the team relinquishes a lead even after the starting pitcher leaves them in a good position. Then his win evaporates with the team's floundering. Where's the justice in that, you might ask? What about the lame hurler who takes over and blows a game? We've not spared him. Patience, our friend.

Tracking a starting pitcher's wins is a way to determine how effective a guy is on the mound. Taken during the course of a career, lots of wins for a pitcher show longevity, consistency, and dominance. As mentioned in Chapter 8, "Hall of Immortality," every pitcher who has won more than 300 games throughout his career has been inducted into the Hall of Fame.

No active pitchers are within striking distance of taking the career wins title from Cy Young. The closest is forty-one-year-old Greg Maddux, who had 347 wins at the close of 2007, his twenty-second season. This is not a shortcoming, but rather highlights the difficulty in comparing players from different eras. Today's best pitchers will have a heck of a time catching up to players from former days like Young and Johnson, primarily because of changes in the pitching rotation, which gives newer pitchers fewer starts and, therefore, fewer opportunities to accumulate wins.

In the early half of the 1900s, it wasn't unheard of for a starting pitcher to lead the league by winning upwards of thirty games. That benchmark slowly dropped, and by the 1950s, a pitcher racking up twenty-five wins in a season was considered quite accomplished. Denny McLain, who pitched for the Detroit Tigers during the 1960s, was a bit of a throwback, at least for a couple of years. In 1968, he nabbed the Cy Young and MVP awards and was the last player to win more than thirty games in a season, something that hadn't been done in thirty-four years. Jackie and her family were in Tiger Stadium for McLain's thirtieth win, though she was too young to remember it. She was plied with ice cream and pretzels and has been informed that it was "the best day of her life." And McLain still had more in him. Within the next month, he finished the season with thirty-one wins and led his Tigers to a World Series Championship. Imagine the rejoicing in the Koney household! Kielbasa for all! But that year was a bit of an anomaly for McLain. The year before he'd won seventeen games and, in 1969, when he earned another Cy Young, he won twenty-four. Pitchers led the league in the 1980s and 1990s with wins that hovered in the high teens and low twenties. The 2006 season marked the first full season in which no starter broke the twenty-win mark in either league. During the coming years, win totals will also be affected by the increasing influx—in both the number and talent—of specialized relief pitchers, who may come in before a starting pitcher has even completed his five innings. Clearly wins are tools that don't paint the whole pitcher picture.

The frequent citing of other statistics benefits from similar scrutiny. Consider strikeouts, for instance. This is a statistic dominated by fast-ballers like Roger Clemens, Walter Johnson, and Nolan Ryan—the strikeout king who retired with a total of 5,714 strikeouts during his twenty-seven years in the majors. Wow. Sounds neat! But what does it mean? That Ryan could deftly hurl fastballs, and he did that for twenty-seven years. No one could throw that many strikeouts in a mediocre career span. By the time he retired he'd also chalked up 324 wins. It's the same thing for Clemens; the forty-four-year-old "Rocket," as Clemens is known, is second in career strikeouts with 4,672 through the 2007 season, his twenty-fourth.

Then, there are those who say it's better to get batters out with tricky pitches that hitters tend to hit into bumbling ground outs, instead of throwing a gazillion fast pitches just trying to get strikeouts. Consider the Hall of Fame's Whitey Ford who, in 1961, won his Cy Young when striking out only 209 batters. Ford pitched for sixteen years, and that was the only year he threw more than 200 strikeouts. That is in stark contrast to Clemens, who threw more than 200 strikeouts in twelve different years, or to Ryan, who threw more than 300 Ks in six different seasons. How tiring. Why wear out your arm throwing three pitches for a strikeout when you can throw one that the batter will pop up for an easy out? We suppose the short answer is that strikeout kings are good at throwing strikes. Simple. Naysayers worry that pitchers employing a strikeout strategy could wear out their arms. Before you know it, they say, the fastballer is on the bus to the glue factory. Though that kind of burnout didn't happen with any of the above-mentioned strikeout wizards, it did for many other famous fastballers.

Red Barrett of the Braves pitched one of the shortest games ever, on August 10, 1944, a 2-0 win over Cincinnati played in one hour, fifteen minutes. One reason it was so short is because Barrett threw a mere fifty-eight pitches and gave up only two base hits. Barrett economically got players out by throwing pitches that batters thought that they could hit. And hit they did. It is just that the majority of the hits ended up as fly balls that sailed into the outfield for a basic catch or ground balls that fielders turned into easy outs. Similarly, whenever a pitcher has few walks or few strikeouts, it makes for a fast game (Barrett had none of each). This is because giving a batter a base on balls requires the time to throw at least four pitches and a strikeout takes at least three. In an equally efficient vein, the Dodgers' Don Drysdale was once asked by his manager to walk a

batter intentionally. Instead of throwing four non-threatening lobs to his catcher and peacefully sending the guy to first, Drysdale instead nailed the unwitting batter on the first pitch. Later, he explained, "Why waste four pitches when one will do?"

Over the course of most of the 1900s, the most common measure of a pitcher's adeptness was his earned run average, or his ERA (pronounced "E-R-A"). While somewhat tricky to calculate, this number reflects the average number of runs opposing teams will score during a typical nine-inning game while a particular pitcher is on the mound. To reduce the concept a little further, ERA sheds light on how good a pitcher is at keeping runners from getting on base. Certain runs are called "earned" because the batter got on base by fault of the pitcher, as opposed to a fielding error. If a batter gets a hit, for example, it is considered the pitcher's fault, as crazy as it may seem. If that same batter scores, the run would be an "earned run," which is then used to calculate the pitcher's ERA. As you can imagine, most runs are earned. Pitchers with lower numbers are supposedly better pitchers than those with higher numbers. If a pitcher has a 2.15 ERA ("two-fifteen") then it is predicted that he will allow a couple runs to score, maybe a little more, maybe a little less, during the course of an entire game. A way to determine whether a pitcher's ERA is considered good, or not, is by thinking how many games are won when the other team scores, using the case of the pitcher with the 2.15 ERA, about two runs. It's likely that if a pitcher can pitch a complete game and give up only two runs, his team is in a good position to win and will likely do so.

But we know that contemporary pitchers rarely complete entire games. No worries, statisticians have a fix for that. If a pitcher leaves the game after pitching three innings and has given up three earned runs, then his ERA for that game would be 9.00 ("nine"). This is calculated by assuming that, had the pitcher stayed in for the full nine innings, he would have continued along in this despicable fashion. If three runs are scored in three innings, the math says the team will score nine runs in nine innings. A pitcher would not be in the major leagues for long at that pace. Well, unless his name is Jose Lima, who had a 9.87 ERA in 2006 while pitching for New York Mets. That's more than one earned run per inning! Okay, okay, that's not fair. Lima, who in the late 1990s was a pitcher with a promising future in the majors, threw in only two games in 2006. Anyone can have a bad week, right? So, for the sake of argument, we'll throw out the 2006 numbers

and go back a year. Let's see. . . . In 2005, Lima had a 6.99 ERA. Ouch. We'd tell you to do the math but, in this case, the math would be wrong. The math tells us that Lima shouldn't be a major league pitcher. And he's not, anymore. But we're softies for a comeback, kid.

There's a lot of focus on ERAs. Is it misguided? With bad ones, perhaps. But when someone has a good one, especially over the course of a year with ample opportunity to pitch, the stat is a fairly accurate assessment. We all know that pitchers are not the only ones responsible when a runner scores. Sure, the guy slipped up and allowed someone to get on base, or worse, hammer a home run, but pitchers are not expected to throw perfect games all the time. We also know that even perfect games take significant contributions from the other fielders.

However, much like the win stat, a pitcher's ERA number does normally coincide with his ability, even if the specific number is somewhat skewed. It is important to remember that the ERA is a statistic intended to average out a pitcher's ability over many games during a season or career. Sometimes, you'll see ERAs that reflect how a pitcher does in a certain month, in an attempt to analyze whether a pitcher performs better in the early spring months or in the heat of the summer. And, like other statistics, comparing ERAs from different eras lacks significance without adding more to the canvas.

Take the dead ball era of the early 1900s. Several things contributed to hitters' woes during this period. Among these were larger stadiums and a change in rules that made the first two foul balls be counted as strikes so batters had fewer chances to get a hit. Pitchers routinely doctored baseballs. And, as mentioned when we wrote about the Ray Chapman tragedy, owners tried to cut down on costs by recycling baseballs, which quickly became haggard. Batters had a hard time just seeing the baseball through all the residual scuff and dirt. When they could pick the ball out and finally get a good hit, the ball wouldn't snap off the bat because it had become so soft, misshapen, and worn from overuse.

Pitchers like Hall of Famers Christy Mathewson and Cy Young pounced and batters floundered. When Young came onboard in the 1890s, the game was still struggling to find a place for pitchers while also working to ensure hitting didn't suffer. During his first ten years, Young's ERA was often above 3.00, which meant he would, in theory, give up about three runs during a complete game. Not bad. However, in 1901 his ERA

dropped considerably and stayed below 2.00 for much of his career. This dramatic change coincided with the beginning of the dead ball era. When Young retired, his career ERA over twenty-two years was 2.63 which, while impressive, is still heavily weighed down by that first decade before the dead ball era. The Hall of Fame's Christy Mathewson began in 1900 and pitched seventeen years—all dead ball years. When all was said and done, his career ERA was 2.13. His best year, if you base that on his lowest ERA, was in 1909 when his average was 1.14 and the league's pitchers averaged 2.59.

Walter Johnson came to the game in the gory glory days of the dead ball era, taking off with a 1.88 ERA in 1907 and thanking the baseball gods for his good fortune. Well, that was until 1920, when balls were regularly replaced and Babe Ruth, having climbed down from his pitcher's perch, had settled into his role as a big hitter. And he brought friends. Soon, the power-hitting game was back in style. Though still well below the league average, Johnson's ERA bonked; in 1919 it was 1.49 and in 1921 it was 3.51. Until the end of his career in 1927, his average ERA was about 3.0.

As the game changed so did ERAs. When Ruth made his mark on the game, hitters were the belles of the ball. After the 1930s, ERAs stabilized somewhat and the league seemed finally to reach a balance between hitting and pitching until the mid-1960s, when the scales briefly tipped in favor of the pitchers. It was brief only because the league's henchmen swooped in, reduced the strike zone—making it preferable to hitters—and lowered the mound. The latter change gave pitchers less leverage, making their curveballs less effective. Soon, pitcher ERAs climbed back up.

To counter the inherent era-induced bias of the ERA, statisticians recently developed other numbers such as "adjusted" ERAs and the WHIP. Adjusted ERAs take into account whether the pitcher plays in a hitter's or pitcher's park and then compares the performance to his pitching peers. The WHIP is a figure that emerged to isolate better a pitcher's talent at something that he has more control over: players getting on base. This number combines walks (W) and hits (H), then divides that number by the total number of innings pitched (IP).

As diligent as baseball statisticians are at creating numbers to level the comparative playing field throughout the game's history, they just can't keep the game from fluctuating. In the span of 100 years, the changes became almost comical—and often maddedning to pitching staffs—to

track. Changes affected even ballpark design. Newer, bigger ballparks were built. Then smaller ones came along. Then they were big again, but with a "small feel." Strike zones got taller, then shorter and wider, then narrower and taller. Yet the umpires calling balls and strikes didn't seem to get the memos. The height of the pitcher's mound varied, affecting pitching statistics—for better or worse—with every adjustment. Baseballs changed. The hitters changed! They started downing protein drinks and carving their bodies on Nautilus machines equipped with fancy sensors. They recharged sore bodies with spa treatments that would make Ty Cobb blush. They reversed the course of aging muscles by popping pills and slathering themselves with questionable creams.

Recently my friend's father died. She was grieving and there was nothing I could do. Some friends gave us their tickets above the dugout, and I had one extra. I asked my bereaved friend to join us, and saw her heal before my eyes, between home plate and first.

—Sally, 46

CHAPTER 29

Send in the Clowns

In the early days of baseball, when a pitcher normally pitched entire games, there was little use for a backup pitcher. The backup guy was often a fielder who would come in to pitch in a pinch. This was when the team's regular starter was injured, too tired, deathly ill, or maybe had to run back home to help his dad with the farm.

Changes in the game led to an increased demand on pitchers' arms. Completing games became more strenuous and happened less frequently. When a starting pitcher was unable to finish a game, someone had to relieve him and take over the pitching duties. It was during the 1930s that managers became more at ease with replacing a tired or flailing pitcher with a relief pitcher who was expected to make things better. It happened infrequently, at first, and wasn't until the early 1950s that most managers embraced the idea of having a full-time reliever or two on the pitching staff. Initially, the jobs went to aging starting pitchers who just didn't have the stuff to compete as starters anymore.

A manager may call for a replacement pitcher for a number of reasons and at any time during a game. These days, a starting pitcher may be limited to the number of pitches he is allowed to throw in a game so that his

pitching arm is preserved for future starts. In this case, a reliever is called in to replace the starter once he has reached his predetermined pitch count, which could be any number, really, depending on the pitcher and what kind of shape he is in. If a starting pitcher is coming off an injury, a manager may treat him gently, having him pitch for a brief time, maybe only a few innings, to help him get back into the groove of things. If the pitcher is feeling his normal, healthy self, his pitch count may be set at around 100 pitches. Or there may be no limit. Usually, when a pitcher begins to show signs of struggling by giving up a few hits, for example, the manager will likely visit the mound to see if he's ready to come out of the game, regardless of what his pitch count is. Sometimes this is a negotiation between the manager and pitcher. Sometimes the pitcher is summarily yanked.

As often as not, a relief pitcher replaces another reliever. This may happen because, while some relievers pitch best in the fifth and sixth innings, others seem to perform best in the seventh and eighth innings. These would be called "middle relievers" because they are used . . . drum roll, please . . . in the middle of the game. Some relievers are very specialized; there are those who bask in the challenge of being called in to the game when there are two outs, two runners on base, and a lefty is at the plate, and there are others who are unbeatable when it's a Saturday night in Chicago and the wind-chill factor is high. A manager may pull an otherwise effective pitcher because he has another pitcher who is good at pitching to the batter who has just come up to the plate. In some cases, such specialists are brought into the game to pitch to only one batter. Then he is replaced with yet another reliever when the at bat is finished, regardless of whether it resulted in an out, a hit, or a home run.

And just as some pitchers are better at starting games, others are better at finishing them. This other breed of pitcher is powerful and dominant but lacks endurance—a requirement to fill the starter position. When a team has a tenuous lead going into the ninth inning, the manager likely pulls whoever is pitching and replaces him with a relief pitcher. But this time it will be with his super special reliever, specifically reserved for this type of situation. These pitchers are called "closers." In many cases, if he doesn't let the lead slip through his fingers, the closer is credited with a "save," a torturous statistic fashioned in 1969.

The "bullpen" is the place where relief pitchers wait to be called into action. Often the bullpen is located in the outfield, behind the fences,

though sometimes it is along the foul lines. It is where the guys spit a lot of sunflower seeds, play jokes, and, in general, where much of nothing good happens. But when a manager makes the "call to the bullpen," the fans soon see one of the relievers put down his toys, straighten his hat, and start throwing a baseball around, all serious-like. He's warming up, getting reading for his turn on the mound. Additionally, the term "bullpen" is synonymous with a team's relief pitching staff and the backup catchers who practice with them.

Starting pitchers may become relievers as they age but, more recently, many guys start as relief pitchers and stay in that position their entire careers. Sparky Lyle never started a game in his sixteen years with five different teams, and never seemed to mind, once saying, "Why pitch nine innings when you can get just as famous pitching two?" It all worked out pretty well, we'd say, fetching him a World Series victory and the Cy Young award while playing for the Yankees in 1977.

Signed by the majors in 1960, Mike Marshall finally made his pitching debut with Detroit seven years later. At the time, he was a freshly minted Michigan State University graduate holding a master's degree in physical education. Initially signed as an infielder, he floundered around the league as a pitcher for three years until he hit his stride and became an official closer for Montreal in 1971. Marshall quickly earned the name "Iron Mike" for his workhorse resilience. By the end of his 1974 season with the Dodgers, Marshall had pitched as many innings as some starting pitchers and had become the first relief pitcher to take home the Cy Young award. He retired in 1981, having played for nine different teams, all while working toward his doctorate in exercise physiology. College boy.

As the closer position became more specialized, the "save" stat began to identify pitchers in this role. Trevor Hoffman holds the major league record for saves, accumulating 524 in fifteen seasons with the San Diego Padres. In nine of those years he rang up an incredible forty or more saves. His predecessor in career saves, Lee Smith, had 478 before retiring from his eighteen-year career. Smith also is among the leaders in career "blown saves," a statistic that emerged to hold closers accountable for their blunders. Smith has 103 blown saves, and Hoffman has sixty-three. Told you we wouldn't spare them.

It is not lost on today's hitters that, back in the day, hitters used to rely on being able to "figure out" a pitcher. This may mean knowing what the

pitcher tends to throw, how well he's throwing it, and the speed at which is is thrown. Or it could mean figuring out what the pitcher is about to throw, much like the way poker players try to figure out an opponent's "tells." To help them do this, hitters need a couple of at bats to get a feel for the pitcher that day. The abundant use of relief staffs makes this familiarization nearly obsolete. Batters rarely see a pitcher three times in a game, which makes it tough on them. Maybe this type of disarmament is what Philadelphia manager Larry Bowa had in mind when his team played the Mets on September 11, 2004. During the course of the thirteen-inning game, the Phillies used ten different pitchers. The Mets returned fire with eight of their own but still lost, 11-9.

While some relievers take their jobs very seriously, waiting for the call that will spring them into action, others take their joke-making seriously. Bullpens, after all, are often celebrated for their pranks and supreme idiocy. Moe Drabowsky was a colorful Polish-born pitcher who began his career in 1956 as a starter. By the time he was traded to Baltimore, just in time to get his 1966 World Series ring, Drabowsky had become a full-time reliever. A known practical jokester, he once used the bullpen phone to place a dinner order, which was delivered to the bullpen during the game. And the fun didn't stop there. Not only did he send a rookie reporter on a search for a "left-handed bat," Drabowsky liked to give the "hot foot," a trick where he would attach a lit book of matches to someone's shoe. The victim would fidget around, trying to maintain a level of composure, until he noticed his shoe was on fire. Drabowski was also responsible for sticking snakes in teammates' lockers, uniforms, and shaving kits and enjoyed putting sneezing powder in the air vents leading to the opposing team's locker room. Just like the stuff you see in *Mission Impossible*; move over, Ethan Hunt!

In 1987, after Drabowsky retired from working as a minor league coach for the White Sox, he told a reporter that ball players didn't seem to have as much fun as they did in the old days. He blamed big egos and money. "Players seem to be more serious, now," he said. "I would tend to believe they don't have as much fun."

I remember going with my Dad to the A's game in the '70s when they won the pennant. Years later, I went to pick my elementary-school-age daughter up from school, and she wasn't there. I became worried! But then the director told me that my Dad had picked her up early and had taken her to the baseball game. Fifteen years later I found out that she got lost going to the bathroom during that game. It was their secret because I was already mad at the fact that he had taken her from school! But that's love.... of baseball, that is.

—Diane, 48

CHAPTER 30

The Battery

Ace starters or second-rate relievers couldn't do their jobs without someone behind the plate making sure their good pitches are caught and their bad ones are made to look like good pitches. We have already talked a little bit about what makes a good catcher. Some catchers unselfishly throw their bodies in front of burly men trying to score. Some throw like Great Aunt Julia trying not to spill her gin and tonic. Others are quiet thinkers. In many cases, a catcher's importance to a team isn't based solely on his offensive statistics or whether he can throw out a guy trying to steal second. Another factor to take into consideration is his role as a partner with the pitcher. Together, they make up the team's "battery."

Since the ball gets to the plate in the blink of an eye, a catcher has to signal for a certain throw so that he will be ready to catch the pitch when it comes in. Otherwise, many pitches would whiz past to the backstop. The signals a catcher gives to the pitcher can be different throughout the game, based on the count, batter, or game situation. Sometimes one finger down means a fastball. Maybe two means a curveball. Three fingers could be an ice pack for his ailing knees. Sometimes a gesture like waving his mitt or making a fist is the agreed upon sign for a pitch.

Back in the early days of the game, pitchers signaled to catchers what they planned to throw, which made it easy for opposing players to figure out what pitch to expect. After all, the same information that makes it possible for a catcher to catch a ball also makes it possible for a hitter to hit the ball. Soon it became important to keep the signs—and pitches—secret. Because of this, the catcher took over the task of signaling for a pitch, usually from between his legs when in the crouch position behind the plate. This made it more difficult for opponents, coaches, and hitters to see and then try to decipher the signals.

Given this obstacle, some teams got creative about stealing signs. The 1951 New York Giants ran an elaborate system that involved a telescope behind centerfield, buzzers, bells, and gestures—all in order to steal signs from the opposing team's catcher. This shady home-field advantage is often thought of as the force behind the team's unlikely hurdle of a thirteen-game late-season deficit, which culminated in beating the Brooklyn Dodgers in a best-of-three-games playoff for the National League pennant. In the final, dramatic Game Three of the series against the Dodgers, the Giants' Bobby Thomson hit a spectacular game-ending homer, famously known, in baseball, as the "shot heard around the world." Thomson denies that he received any information about that pitch which ended the game.

In addition to giving and disguising signals, the catcher has to catch each pitch. Sounds fair enough, but it's not as easy as it looks. He must not let the blazing fastballs get past, though some inevitably do, either because the pitcher threw a wild pitch or the catcher made a mistake. Sometimes it's both, as in the case with a knuckleball pitcher. Knuckleball pitches aren't officially wild pitches, though they are often indisputably untamed.

The Red Sox organization didn't realize how important Doug Mirabelli, their backup catcher of four years, had become until they traded him to the Padres during the 2005 off season. They found out quickly. By the end of April 2006, Mirabelli's replacement, Josh Bard, was having difficulty corralling starter Tim Wakefield's knuckleballs. In his first five games, the pitcher had an abysmal 1-4 record (one win, four losses) and Bard had already allowed seven passed balls in those five games. The duo had not meshed.

So Boston executives called their *amigos* at the Padres and inquired about returning Mirabelli to the Red Sox. As it turned out, San Diego

had acquired superstar catcher Mike Piazza, sans mustache, and was giving Mirabelli less playing time than originally planned.

The two teams worked out a quickie deal. The Red Sox wanted Mirabelli to report to Boston for Wakefield's next start. Not only did this tight transaction require a private jet, but it also called for a police escort from the tarmac at Boston's Logan Airport directly to Fenway Park. The catcher's uniform was even waiting for him in the car and Mirabelli changed while the entourage sped through downtown Boston. As some of you may know, this is not a ride not for the squeamish. Total time from the tarmac at Logan to first pitch from Wakefield to the Yankees leadoff hitter Johnny Damon: twenty-five minutes. With his trusty catching companion behind the plate, Wakefield racked up three wins that month.

Bard was a good catcher but allowed too many Wakefield pitches to pass him. Passed balls can make the pitcher lose his confidence. When a catcher lets a ball pass him, he has to scramble behind the umpire and home plate to retrieve it, and bad things can happen on the field. If there are runners on base, this complicates matters because, while the catcher is collecting the passed ball, runners could be heading to the next base.

Advancing runners were the least of catcher Mickey Owen's problems during Game Four of the 1941 World Series against the Yankees. There was no one on base, and the Brooklyn Dodgers team was one out shy of tying the best-of-seven-games series 2-2, when reliever Hugh Casey struck out the Yankees' Tommy Henrich for the last out of the game. Or so it seemed. As Henrich finished his swing, the ball got away from the Brooklyn catcher. Owen scurried for the ball as it rolled toward the backstop, and Henrich took first base easily. This mistake by the catcher was scored a "passed ball." The error also called into play an obscure rule that allowed Henrich to reach base. This rule is the sixth of seven ways for a batter to get on base and comes into play when the catcher drops the third strike. An alert runner takes the opportunity and heads to first, like Henrich did. Brooklyn fans were not as astute. Elated, they thought that their team had struck out the last batter, won the game, and evened the series. Not so. Rather, the Brooklyn reliever next faced Joe DiMaggio, who snapped a base hit into right field, leading the Yankees to a four-run ninth inning and a 7-4 win. The next night the Yankees claimed the World Series.

Pitchers have come up with some nifty ideas to change the game, but not all inventions come from the mound, although they inspire most of

the rest, like a special catcher's mitt to absorb the sting of a fastball. In the 1960s, an oversized catcher's mitt was designed so that catchers could handle the unwieldy pitches from the Orioles' Hoyt Wilhelm, the Hall of Fame knuckleballer. Today, Boston's Mirabelli uses a softball catcher's mitt. It was almost a century before, however, when injuries from fastballs and tipped balls drove the need to devise the catcher's chest protector. About the same time, a Harvard University player adapted the gear used in fencing to create the first catcher's mask. Eventually more pads were added, then shin guards, helmets—the works. Spare no expense! Innovation at its best. Creative advancements aside, it should be noted that all the gear catchers wear is often referred to as their "tools of ignorance."

Disregard for aches and pains aside, good catchers are valued around the league for their knowledge of strategy, a batter's strengths and weaknesses, and for their field awareness. The catcher's view of the field helps, for instance, when a baserunner is getting the itch to steal second. In that case, the catcher may quickly signal for a "pitchout." This is a pitch thrown fast and high, supposedly outside the reach of the batter so that the catcher can spring up from his crouch, catch the ball, and be in a good position to make the throw to get the runner trying to steal second out. This pitch can look like one thrown for an intentional walk, the difference being the pace of the pitch. An intentional walk is often easily thrown.

Sometimes a batter can thwart the pitchout play and protect his base-stealing teammate. On June 1, 2004, the Mets and Philadelphia were tied 1-1 going into the tenth inning when Todd Zeile, the third baseman for the Mets, came up to bat and jolted the game with an unusual play. The team's leadoff hitter, Kazuo Matsui, was on first with no outs and was planning a steal attempt with Zeile at the plate. When "Kaz" took off for second, Zeile intentionally swung wildly at the pitchout throw, looking a little silly but distracting the catcher enough to make him miss the throw to second. Now, with a runner on second, Zeile singled to centerfield, scoring Matsui and breaking the tie. The Mets went on to score two more runs that inning and won the game, 4-1. See what can happen when runners get into scoring position? Gus Schmelz was certainly onto something.

Catchers play an important role in the game when they decide on a pitch to recommend, whether a pitchout or a curveball. A good catcher knows not only the strengths and weaknesses of his opponents but also those of the pitcher with whom he is working. It is said that catchers, using

this knowledge, "call the game." This means that much of the strategy of when to throw a fastball, or whether to throw another right afterwards or to follow with a curveball, comes from the catcher. While the ultimate responsibility of each pitch rests with the pitcher, when the battery does a good job at changing the pace of the game and unsettling the batters, it is said that the catcher "called a good game."

When a catcher is new to the league, the team, or a certain pitcher, the game might be called from the "bench," the dugout where the coach signals to the catcher who, in turn, signals the selected pitch to the pitcher. Whew! That's a flurry of signals to master and hide from the opponents. Conversely, some veteran pitchers like to call their own game, having discussed with the catcher beforehand his strategy for the day. But the catcher still sends the signals to the pitcher.

You'll occasionally see a pitcher shaking his head at the catcher. This is called, somewhat obviously, "shaking off" the catcher. The pitcher does this until the catcher signals for a pitch that the pitcher feels good about. You may even see a pitcher shaking off two or three calls. Maybe the pitcher thinks the hitter will send that certain pitch out of the park. Or maybe the pitcher doesn't think he can throw that pitch well enough on this outing. Eventually, if the pitcher doesn't get the call that wants, the duo may stop the game and talk about it. This would be one reason for a "mound visit." The catcher calls for a break, or "time," from the umpire and trots out to talk to his pitcher. In the case of shaking off the catcher, the two likely discuss the merits of different pitches and decide on a strategy. Then, the catcher returns to his place, and the game continues.

The Yankees' Lefty Gomez, a Hall of Fame pitcher with a fourteen-year career beginning in 1930 was once visited by his catcher because Gomez kept shaking off the signs to pitch to Jimmie Fox, a frightening power hitter. "What do you want to throw?" asked catcher Bill Dickey. Gomez told his catcher that he didn't want to throw anything. "Maybe he'll get tired of waiting and leave."

Often the manager or pitching coach will accompany the catcher to the mound for a chat to see how the arm's feeling; maybe he's ready to come out. Other times, pitchers are happy to have the catcher to talk to when things get a little dicey. Catchers may also run out to the mound just to break the rhythm of a batter who is nailing long foul balls into the stands. Who knows? The batter could straighten out his next hit and send it clear

over the outfield fence. So the catcher goes out to "ice" the batter. Just to make him *think* about that next pitch.

The catcher also is the one fielder ensconced in enemy territory, tightly sandwiched between the opposing team's batter and the umpire. Who's the guy to talk to? Well, many catchers manage interesting relationships with both the umpire and the batter. The catcher could make nice with the umpires so that maybe, just maybe, the guy will call that next high fastball a strike. Brown-noser? Nah. Smart gamer? Sure.

Some catchers are historically quiet, others are chatty. According to retired umpire Dave Phillips, the Yankees' Thurman Munson was the talkative type. Munson, "habitually talked to everyone, umpires, hitters, whomever," Phillips told *Sporting News* in 2004. "One time, the Yankees were playing the Royals, and [George] Brett finally said to Munson: 'The barbecue is great in Kansas City. No, I haven't gotten married. My golf game is terrible. Now, just let me hit.'" Maybe the chatty catcher is just looking for another way to unnerve the batter. And maybe the catcher doesn't really even need to talk to do that.

You've read already a bit about how catchers put on their fielding armor to keep them glued together until the end of the game. As if they don't have enough physical danger to contend with, catchers sometimes put themselves in harm's way by squatting close to the batter. This is intended to annoy the batter, who can ask that the catcher move back. Or, the batter may choose to fume silently, getting even with the wise guy behind him by smacking him with his bat when the pitch comes. And not only is this legal, it is smart baseball! You see, the onus lies on the catcher to make sure he is not in the way of the batter's swing. This play would fall under the "catcher interference" rule where the batter is given first base, while the catcher is left writhing on the ground wondering why he didn't become a dentist, like his mother wanted. This rule stems from the mean old days when catchers would tip or grab the bat as the batter was about to swing, throwing him off-kilter. "Catcher interference" is the seventh, and final, way a batter can get on base. Got 'em all?

At a recent funeral, my cousin shared a story about his mother, a Red Sox fan. But his dad was a Yankee fan. She wouldn't allow him to watch or listen to those Yankee games inside the house. So Uncle John would go outside to the car and put on the car radio. The moral of this story: Red Sox fans are tenacious!

—Caroline, 55

CHAPTER 31

The Brushback, the Beanball, and the Brain

Some pitchers are well regarded for outwitting batters by using instinct and cunning, instead of sheer brawn. These are guys who control their pitches with pinpoint accuracy and speed, although they sometimes forego the speed on a given pitch, the point being that they can change like a chameleon, which is infuriating to batters. Different pitches, like the fastball, curveball, and forkball, among others, are achieved by placing the fingers in different positions around the baseball. Batters, desperate for a clue as to what pitch to expect, watch the pitcher's hands closely, trying to determine his hand position and, thus, which pitch he will throw. Pitchers work hard to disguise what they are plotting, burying their hands in their gloves until just before the ball is released.

Greg Maddux is a contemporary pitcher who earned his nickname "The Professor" for using his smarts and his muscles to beat batters throughout his twenty-two-year career. He isn't considered a junkballer but, instead, has the uncanny ability to throw fastballs at different speeds, and with "good

motion," which means that the ball sails, tails, or sinks as it approaches the plate. Pitchers can give batters pause when they have the talent to throw with speed *and* motion. Sometimes, it is just enough pause so they don't know when to swing.

"Off speed" pitches are confounding because being able to pick out a pitch early in its delivery is an advantage that batters like to seize. For instance, when a batter sees a pitcher unload a fastball, which he can determine from the way the ball is held, he can brace for something in the way of an 85 mph pitch. It'll get there pretty fast. Guys like Maddux and Mike Mussina, however, are good at disguising pitches. Their hands lie. Based on how they hold the ball, a batter may expect a fastball and prepare to swing away. That's until a 65 mph pitch warbles by for a strike. This talent messes with the batter's rhythm. Hitters don't know what to prepare for in the millisecond it takes for the pitch to arrive and are often foiled by the speed change. And Mussina, like Maddux, throws fastballs with good motion. If a pitcher relies on a scorching 98 mph fastball, it'd better have a little motion or else batters will be able to identify it a mile away and crush it back even farther.

It is interesting that, for a respected "control pitcher," Maddux is nineteenth on the all-time career list of hitting batters with a ball. Just why would he control that ball 131 times into a player's back or arm or anything for that matter? Well, the number has more to do with his longevity than his aimlessness. After all, despite his position on the all-time leader board, the number averages out to only six hit batters per year out of the almost 1,000 that he faces in a given season. Not that it didn't hurt each one of them. It's just that maybe it's not as bad as it seems on stat sheets; fastball pitcher Walter Johnson tops the list with 203 hit batters in as many years as Maddux. Mussina, capable of much harder throws than Maddux, plunked only fifty-two batters through the 2007 season, his seventeenth.

Even though Johnson hit a bunch of guys, some say he really felt badly about it. For one thing, the "Big Train" knew that his fastball could seriously hurt someone, and he took pains not to hit anyone. But, if he was so contrite, why did it happen so often? One theory is that his pitches came in so fast that it was hard for batters to get out of the way, especially those who crowded the plate. Some of the game's best fastballers, such as Clemens, Randy Johnson, and Pedro Martinez, also top the list of pitchers hitting batsmen. Sometimes batters ask for it, choosing to stand close into the

plate so they can see the ball better. The stitching on the ball reveals which way it is spinning—if it's a curveball or fastball—and how fast it's coming. This kind of information comes at a steep fee, obviously.

In the early days of baseball, pitchers would occasionally apologize for hitting a batter. How times have changed! And they changed quickly. By the early 1900s, it was somewhat acceptable to throw the ball "inside" in order to "brush" the batter back from the plate for subsequent pitches and at bats—sort of like sending a warning flare. But sometimes, the warning shot became a shot to the hip. These days, batters still crowd the plate and pitchers still get warnings from umpires for throwing too many dangerous "brushback" pitches.

The Dodgers' Don Drysdale was the king of the brushback pitch. So good was he, in fact, that he brushed back 154 batters with a ball to the body during the course of his fourteen-year career. He missed scads more but, we think, players got the drift. He wanted to own the strike zone above the plate and didn't like anyone stepping into it. What's more, he would blame batters for getting hit. "They crowded the plate and stepped into an inside pitch and hit themselves," he would say. "If you're going to step into the pitch, I refuse to be held accountable. . . . The inside part of the plate is mine too."

Sometimes, when pitchers get really annoyed, they'll throw close to the batter's head as a final warning to step away from the plate. Sometimes pitchers will hit the batter in the head with a pitch. We'd all like to think that such "beanballs" are accidents, but there's really no telling. Sometimes, pitchers are so crazy that they never issue warnings. On May 1, 1974, Dock Ellis of the Pirates opened a game by intentionally hitting the first three Reds batters, though not in their heads, and loading the bases. Then he walked the next batter. But with the bases already loaded, this walk allowed Pete Rose, who was the first batter and was walked around to third base, to score. After the fourth walk and the scored run, Ellis was yanked by his manager. This is the same Dock Ellis, incidentally, who admitted to throwing a no-hitter while on LSD four years earlier. Who knows? Maybe the rest of us are crazy.

In the mid-1960s, hitters started taking throws to the head and brushback pitches personally. Anything that came close or actually hit them would be a matter for some nasty glares, at least, and, occasionally, nastier words. Sometimes, afflicted batters would charge the pitcher's mound,

seeking retribution. A batter usually doesn't make it as far as the pitcher's mound, though. He is tackled from behind by the catcher or stopped by players who leave the dugout to offer support. Sometimes the pitcher runs for cover!

But not on August 4, 1993, when a twenty-six-year-old, big-hitting stud named Robin Ventura was nailed in the back by a 96 mph pitch from Nolan Ryan, who was wrapping up his twenty-seventh, and final, season in the majors. After taking a couple of cursory steps toward first base, Ventura decided it would be a good idea to charge the forty-six-year-old pitcher. You know, give the geezer a little taste of his own medicine. But Ventura was not tackled by the catcher. He was not rescued by his teammates. Approaching the Hall of Fame pitcher, he paused, probably wishing he'd become a dentist. Arriving at the mound unfettered, Ventura found an incredulous Ryan who stuck the youngster in a headlock and pounded on him until someone intervened. Ventura's manager took him out of the game immediately after the scuffle, probably for psychiatric evaluation. He never made it to first base. Ryan pitched four more innings, got the win, and secured a place on highlight reels for eternity.

I like that baseball is truly a team sport, but it is also a sport of individuals. The basic rules have hardly changed in generations. I like that a good catcher can go from a crouching position, to flinging off his gear, catching a ball and getting the runner out at second with a rocket. I like that it is a game of teams against teams, not strictly against the clock. I love the smell of leather, of grass in the sunshine. I like that not all fields have the exact same dimensions or rules. I like the silly games and contests between innings, especially at minor league games. And, it just feels good to swing a bat and hit something, because it is so darn hard to do. How much more room do I have here?

—Ellen, 41

SECTION SIX

Let's Get Organized

It takes some doing to plan all of the runs that will get a team to the playoffs. That's right. After wading through a 162-game regular season, the prize is a postseason juggernaut filled with wild cards, division races, pennant fever, and the Queen Bee of them all: the World Series. At some point a team's pitching game hopefully falls into place because, after all, pitching is what wins championships. Or so it has been said.

But first you must get there. One of the first steps a manager takes to get ready for the season is organizing his players into a nine-person batting order. This is the queue that players wait in each game to have a chance to bat. Knowing who is coming up to bat will help you know why the stadium is starting to buzz with anticipation. If Babe Ruth were coming up with three on base and only one out, you'd have reason to be excited, too—and probably a little freaked out, since he's been dead for more than fifty years.

As for the managers, we would completely understand if, after taking a look at all the different players on his twenty-five man roster, one of the first things he did was roll his eyes and head for the movies. After all, there are millions upon millions of ways to organize a baseball roster into a starting lineup. And most of those permutations aren't going to win any championships. That is, unless you are the 1975 Cincinnati Reds, whose team was so good that it probably wouldn't have mattered had the mascot batted.

In fact, organizing batting orders has become such a compelling topic that an entire school of thought exists, which is dedicated to researching lineups and their ensuing destruction or vindication. High school math students are given batting order problems to solve and dissertations are written about how to rearrange teams. What researchers can't pinpoint, however, is this: When is the lineup tweaked because the manager just has a gut feeling about something? Jimmy's mom is in the stands? Let him play! A rookie got lucky last night? Bench him. Maybe one-time Red Sox manager Joe Morgan got wind that Wade Boggs was served tofu instead of his usual chicken dinner before the game. Oh my. May the heavens open up and bring a rainout!

CHAPTER 32

The Madness to the Method

Throughout baseball's history, managers have tested different methods for organizing the team's mix of power-posting gorillas and sinewy base stealers into the most effective lineup. One idea was to place players in order of batting average, where the guy with the best average hits at the top of the order, or first. Another idea was to pull names out of a hat. Regardless of the chosen course, research has shown that a team's best lineup could favorably change the outcome of several games in a season. Wow. Now, that is big news! Our only question is: Why isn't everyone using this method? You know, the "best lineup" method? Alert the presses!

The basic idea behind the most commonly used system is that a specific place in the lineup requires a specific type of hitter or runner. For example, the first guy in the lineup—the "leadoff" hitter—is often a fast guy who can use his speed to eke out base hits and steal bases. Similarly, many of the top five or six spots in the lineup require specific talent, making certain players a natural fit for those slots.

 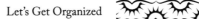

But once managers have some of the "easy" spots filled in the lineup, they look to have specific players hitting before or after certain other players. When you combine this with the idea that some hitters just like batting second while others perform better in the "four hole," or the fourth spot . . . well, it all becomes tricky mental gymnastics. Ultimately, putting together the day's order turns into a convoluted process whereby a manager assembles what he hopes is the optimum mix of the day's most reliable hitters, best runners, and most rested players.

Most managers agree that basing the order on a player's likelihood of getting on base is the best way to arrange things. This means that the first person at bat should be a good hitter and good at getting on base, come hell or high water. This would be someone like Wade Boggs, the Hall of Famer who was a regular leadoff for Boston during the 1980s. The leadoff's combination of talents makes it possible for him to have a high on-base percentage (OBP), which means he gets on base a lot and is the player on the team who is most likely to get on base. When runners get on base, the pitcher feels the pressure, particularly when the guy on base is a threat to steal.

Manager's note to self: Whenever you have a chance to screw with a pitcher's groove, do it.

When you think about the characteristics of the "number-one" hitter, it becomes pretty obvious that he'll have a high OBP—he does whatever he can to get on base. Well, doesn't everyone? Yes, but some are simply better than others at doing it and this guy is likely the best on the team. A player's OBP correlates loosely to batting average, but it is likely higher because this statistic reflects also how often the player got to first base either by a walk or being hit by a pitch, two figures that aren't represented in a player's batting average. You won't normally see the leadoff hit a bunch of home runs because his job is simply to get himself onto base and, eventually, into scoring position.

Leadoff hitters are also notoriously patient batters; they're exceptionally talented at working the count and frustrating pitchers with their tenacity. In some circles, this is called "plate discipline." You have read already about Richie Ashburn's freakish penchant for fouling off pitches into the stands. His fortitude with pitchers also paved the way for the Philadelphia outfielder to get on base via walks, another hallmark of a skilled leadoff hitter that boosts his OBP.

When the leadoff gets on base, it's often up to the next batter to get him into scoring position. But some of the game's best leadoff hitters take pride in getting into scoring position all by themselves. Pete Rose, while not especially speedy, used his notorious grit to stretch would-be singles into extra bases so often that he led the league in doubles five times. Rickey Henderson, arguably the best leadoff hitter in the game's history, used his instincts and brazenness to steal his way into better scoring position 1,402 times. And he stole his way home to score an additional four times. The audacity! Henderson's 1,406 total steals leaves in the dust the previous major league record of 938 set by Hall of Famer Lou Brock, another classic leadoff hitter. Additionally, Henderson flaunted his power swing on occasion, stunning opposing pitchers 297 times with a homer.

But when the leadoff hitter simply gets on first, it is up to the "number-two" hitter to advance the runner into scoring position. There are a number of different ways to advance a runner on base and they range from getting a pedestrian base hit to hitting a sacrifice, which means that he unselfishly surrenders his chance at getting on base so that the runner might have the chance to advance into scoring position. These number-two guys can be classified as an altruistic type; they are typically team players who do what needs to be done for the greater good.

Former Red Sox second baseman Marty Barrett hit in the second spot behind Boggs during much of the 1980s. Barrett seemed to possess the appropriately humble demeanor for this often-unglamorous spot in the lineup. "I sure felt comfortable hitting second," he told *Baseball Digest* in August, 2002. "I could kind of lay in the weeds and be overlooked by the other teams." Nice. Would you like an olive or twist of lemon with your swamp water?

Seriously, these guys are fundamental players, not startlingly different from the leadoff hitter but maybe a little better at connecting with a pitch, whether it is a ball or strike. Hall of Famer Nellie Fox was a number-two hitter for the Chicago White Sox and averaged only one strikeout in every forty-three at bats. This is an astounding figure. In 1953, arguably one of his worst seasons, he struck out only eighteen times. Compare that to Reggie Jackson, who averaged a strikeout in every four at-bats, which is about one every game. Fox's talent, much like other "two-hole" batters, enabled him to perform well in a "hit and run" situation, another way to advance the runner that was discussed in the Chapter 17, "Sacrifice." The number-two hitter also benefits from more power than the leadoff, possibly hitting the ball to

 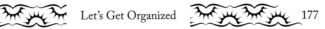

deep right field so that the speedy baserunner has the opportunity to take third base on a base hit, taking advantage of the long and difficult throw from the right field corner.

By the time the "number-three" hitter comes up, ideally there are two runners on base and there are no outs. The third batting slot regularly falls to the best overall hitter on the team. It's a position that calls for the ability to hit for average and power, meaning that it is likely that the three-hole not only gets on base a lot but that his powerful swing ensures multiple-base hits and home runs. Some of baseball's greats, like Ted Williams, Babe Ruth, Hank Aaron, and Willie Mays come to mind. The three-hole batter is an all-around team player who is not only capable of doing what is best for the team but willing to make tough decisions, maybe even if it negatively impacts his statistics. Because of these characteristics, many number-three hitters are regarded in the clubhouse and in the press corps as good guys. Well, Williams had a bit of an edge to him.

Roberto Clemente was the consummate third batter during much of the 1960s. He managed a career .317 batting average while scrapping out 440 doubles, 166 triples, and holding his own in the home-run category. At his last at bat of the 1972 season, his eighteenth and final year with the Pittsburgh Pirates, Clemente reached exactly 3,000 career hits—a weighty benchmark reserved for baseball legends. He died in a plane crash the following New Year's Eve delivering food to earthquake victims in Nicaragua. The following season, MLB renamed the Commissioner's Award, which was awarded to the player who displayed commitment to the community and helping others, the Roberto Clemente Award.

Then there is the baseball *cognoscenti* contention that many number-three hitters have inflated batting averages because of the powerful hitters who are likely to bat next in the order. Three-holers are protected, in a sense, because pitchers know that the next batter is often capable of hitting the long ball. Depending on the situation—if the first two batters are on base, for example, and the number-four hitter is a home run threat—pitchers are disinclined to allow another runner on base. Another runner could load the bases and set the number-four hitter up for a grand slam. Faced with this conundrum, pitchers are often forced to throw the third batter pitches that he is apt to hit.

What's that you said?! Pitchers want these great hitters to hit the ball?!? Sure, it sounds like a boneheaded strategy, but pitchers hope these guys put

the ball into play for a ground out, fly out, or the gold-standard double-play. Since the best players get a hit only one every three chances, maybe it's not such a bad gamble. Or maybe the pitcher can trick the batter into striking out. Number-three hitters may be great, but they are human. Nonetheless, this pitching strategy is often futile, as you can see by their high batting averages and OBP, because these skilled batters often do the damage they are supposed to do.

The first three hitters are expected to "set the table" for the fourth batter by getting on base, advancing the runners, or loading the bases. The fourth slot is reserved for the "cleanup guy" because, with hopefully the bases loaded, he is expected to clear the bases. Additionally, having three good hitters in front of him, this batter is sheltered from some of the vagaries of the game, rarely facing tricky and stressful situations such as when there are two outs and no men on base.

Lou Gehrig was one of the most famous cleanup hitters of all time when he played for the New York Yankees during the 1920s and 1930s. When the bases were loaded, Gehrig hit twenty three home runs, or "grand slams," over the course of his career. Now, that's clutch! These number-four sluggers are often measured by their slugging percentage, which is a statistic we first discussed in Chapter Ten, "Hitting the Basics." Gehrig's lifetime slugging percentage is .632 and his seventeen-year career batting average was .340. When he knocked in forty-seven home runs in 1927, his slugging percentage that year was .765.

The fifth spot could be considered a second power spot in many respects. This batter would be someone slightly less reliable with the big hits than the number-four hitter, or he could be someone who has spent time in the fourth slot and got moved down the lineup because the team acquired a more powerful hitter. Sometimes this move will come with age.

Brooks Robinson was the Baltimore Orioles' stellar third baseman during the team's hot streak in the late 1960s and early 1970s, when the franchise won two World Series in four appearances. His movement through the batting order is emblematic of how some power hitters switch around, going up and down the order. As long as they are able to produce offensively, these hitters are valued by the team.

As the number-four power hitter, Brooksie, as we like to call him, batted after Frank Robinson and helped lead the team to its 1966 World Series win, beating the Los Angeles Dodgers in four games. During the next two

years, however, the team's studly, big-hitting first baseman Boog Powell started batting cleanup on occasion, and Brooksie started working his way down the lineup.

Still producing offensively for the team, Brooks was also still winning Gold Gloves—sixteen in a row—for his skill at third base. By the team's 1970 World Series-winning season, he was ensconced in the sixth spot for most of the season, though manager Earl Weaver moved him back up to the fifth spot for the World Series. Seems like the move worked: during the series win over the Cincinnati Reds, the thirty-three-year-old Brooksie had a .810 slugging percentage and was awarded the series MVP.

After the top half of the lineup, if there is another power hitter handy, he's apt to go in the sixth spot. Otherwise, the last four slots in the lineup are sometimes organized in descending order by batting average, trading offensive skill for defensive ability. These players are also likely to be substituted for in the late innings of a game, when the manager needs a stroke of strategic genius. Over the course of a season, these guys see fewer at bats than the starters at the top of the lineup, which is exactly what managers want: less-skilled batsmen seeing fewer pitches.

Four-time All-Star catcher Bob Boone played for three different teams, averaging .254, during his nineteen-year career. Despite his low average, Boone was in the lineup most games, albeit relegated to the bottom half. In 1980, when his Philadelphia team beat the Kansas City Royals in the World Series, Boone showed for an admirable 141 games and 480 at bats. At the other end of the lineup, Pete Rose, Boone's teammate, played the full 162 games and accumulated 655 at bats; the difference in at bats is mostly due to Rose's assignment to either the first or second spot in the lineup. One of the game's best defensive catchers, Boone won the Gold Glove seven times, making him a necessary fixture behind the plate—and in the batting order.

The idea of a traditional lineup was skewed in the American League when, in 1973, it adopted the designated hitter rule, which we'll discuss later in this section. This allowed AL teams to replace the worst hitter, often the pitcher, with a better one. However, the National League never adopted the designated hitter and still normally reserves the ninth slot for pitchers. Pitchers are often the worst hitters because they spend so much time honing their pitching skills that they can afford little time for practice in the batting cage. Managers want them to throw pitches, not see them.

I grew up watching the Cubs with my mom. Being one of twelve children, I played baseball every summer. No matter where I lived in the United States, I was able to watch a great Cubs game. And when they hit a home run, I'd call my mom and yell, "Did you see it?!"

—*Anonymous*

CHAPTER 33

And If That Doesn't Work

$\mathcal{M}$anagers are often pushed to the brink when looking for a way for their teams to jell. They may even try to get out of a slump or eke out another few runs by rearranging the batting order. A common arrangement is to alternate left-handed hitters with right-handed ones. Another idea is to shuffle the order by putting the team's highest-average hitter at the top of the order. This is the same guy who is likely batting in the number-three spot in the previously discussed lineup. The reasoning behind having your highest-average hitter batting first is that, as the game moves on and the batting order has been circulated a couple times, players who start at the top of order will hit at least as often—and likely more often—than any other player on the roster. This is just what managers want: better batsmen seeing more pitches.

Manager Connie Mack had a hard time finding a groove with his Philadelphia A's. The team stunk from 1935 to 1943, ending up in one of the last two spots in the American League every single year. Exasperated,

in June, 1939, he threw out his well-considered batting order. As the story goes, he wrote all of his players' batting averages in descending order on the back of a cocktail napkin. This new batting order brought his team out of a tailspin. But even though the team had their best month of the season, the idea was scrapped.

To further build on the theme that only crummy teams get so desperately creative, we introduce a fresh-faced manager named Bobby Bragan. In he walks, dragging his 1956 Pittsburgh Pirates. The team was preposterously pathetic, and, to be generous, the manager was trying to bring it out of an eight-year tailspin by buying into Mack's idea. The team did marginally better during the short-lived experiment but still finished the season with a .429 winning percentage.

Now that we've worked through what makes a sound lineup, or at least what makes it somewhat defensible, full disclosure necessitates that we tell you there is some debate as to whether any of this matters. Many researchers question the validity of putting together a batting order based on OBP, batting average, mothers' maiden names, or anything else for that matter. What we're getting at is that some people think there is no such thing as a "best lineup."

Could it be that lovingly organized batting orders score no more runs than those ordered randomly? According to these baseball researchers, yes. Furthermore, they assert that a random order may actually be the best method because it can remove player inconsistency. So, wait—are they saying that there is a best order, and that the best order is no order? Man, where are the shots of whiskey and those little standup figures when you need them?

The basic premise of any non-method is that a perfectly suitable lineup can be devised by a barrel of monkeys or even Billy Martin, the erstwhile New York Yankee manager. When his team was embroiled in a nasty losing streak in 1977, this manager was brought to his knees. Out of desperation, he randomly picked the lineup out of his hat. This is the same guy who reportedly paid his pitcher $100 to bean a batter and, later, punched out a Minnesota marshmallow salesman, to the tune of fifteen stitches and a night in jail. Heck, he pretty much fought with everyone. But, while Martin may have been crazy, it doesn't mean he was wrong.

Having a team like the Mariners, win or lose, you still support them and become part of the team with all of the love and devotion of the whole team. They are sort of like my family. I have been a single mom for many years and so much enjoy taking my eleven-year-old son. Yes, it is expensive, but it's so cool to have my little boy experience history in the making. I literally cry every last game of the season . . . I live for baseball and can't wait for [the] next season.

—*Suzette, 49*

CHAPTER 34

Designated for Assignment

$\mathscr{A}$ few paragraphs back, we mentioned that the American League has the use of a position called the designated hitter (DH), and that the National League never adopted this position. The DH is a player whose usefulness is based solely on his offensive brawn. His hitting is so valuable that he is given a spot in that day's lineup as a special batter, although he does not have a position in the field. Instead, this hitter is substituted into the lineup for the weakest hitter, usually the pitcher. However, the DH is not inserted into the same lower-tier slot that the weaker one would occupy, but rather, the DH is moved up in the order because his skills befit that of a batter in the top half of the lineup.

In the late 1960s, pitching had once again become king, and team owners, fearful that fans would get bored with low-scoring games, scrambled to find ways to negate this defensive power. Among other league changes, such as lowering the pitcher's mound, the DH was regarded as a solution to the league's offensive sufferings. Charlie Finley, the eccentric Oakland A's

owner, was among the DH's strongest advocates, saying that the "average fan comes to the park to see action, home runs. I can't think of anything more boring than to see a pitcher come up [to bat]."

To some fanfare, the American League adopted the DH in 1973. Some baseball fans decry the DH as a slight to the game's venerable tradition and look to the National League as the purer of the two leagues because it never recognized the position. Initially, the DH rule was supposed to be in effect for only three years, but the payoff—the offensive boom and eleven-percent-attendance boost—was too great to ignore.

Harmon "Killer" Killebrew was wrapping up his twenty-two-year Hall of Fame career, which he mostly spent with the Minnesota Twins, when the DH was instituted. For the thirty-seven-year-old Killer, the DH came not a moment too soon. His batting average had taken a hit, as had his playing time, yet he was still splitting time between the third spot in the batting order and the powerful cleanup spot. Killebrew hit 573 career homers and led the league in home runs six times, an unrivaled dominance for the time. He was also one of only four players to clear the towering left-field roof of Tiger Stadium. In 1975, Killebrew joined the Kansas City Royals and filled the DH position. With their new DH, the team moved up three spots from the previous year's final standings and posted its best year since the franchise formed in 1969. Coincidence? Since the Killer didn't clear the Mendoza Line that year, we'd say, yes, it was probably a coincidence.

All AL teams have a regular DH that they use in most games. If the regular DH isn't in the batting order, he rarely, if ever, plays the field. DHs are originally drafted into the MLB as position players and move to fill the DH role based on the team's needs. Sometimes this is because the player has aged and lost a step on the field but is still formidable at the plate. The DH slot is a perfect haven for the worn and battered bodies of the over thirty-five set, like Killebrew. And, for many of us fans, the DH gives us more time to enjoy beloved players who may have become a little creaky. In the NL, where there is no DH, older players prolong careers by becoming first basemen because the position isn't as grueling as others in the field. But, since nothing is ever written in stone, after becoming a DH, players will occasionally take the field, such as when interleague play started in 1997 and teams abided by the home team's league rules. That is, AL pitchers are in the batting order when they play in NL stadiums and NL teams get to use a DH while in AL parks.

All-Star Edgar Martinez came up to play with Seattle in 1987 as a twenty-four-year-old third baseman with soft hands but settled into the DH spot by 1995. That year he became the only DH to win a batting title. For the remainder of his eighteen-year career, he played DH almost exclusively. Other teams have players "platoon" the DH role. For example, a right-handed hitter and a left-handed hitter will split the position, each playing DH when the manager sees fit for a strategic move requiring one batter over the other. The most obvious effect the DH has on the lineup is that the National League's notoriously weak-hitting pitchers are required to bat. The absence of the DH means the NL can't take advantage of the additional firepower that the position brings. Conversely, this also means that AL teams have one extra good hitter on their roster. This neatly corresponds with the slightly higher batting averages that AL teams have had since the adoption of the DH.

I like the pace and the strategy of baseball. It can be really sleepy, really exciting, or really tense with lots of drama. The pace of the game is what creates the different types of energy. Plus, it seems like you can be a professional baseball player but can still be out until 4:00 A.M. pounding beers the night before a big game.

—Jennifer, 38

Chapter 35

Tweak This

There isn't a manager around who isn't getting harassed about his lineup, whichever one he opts to implement. Use the veteran with the sagging average? Switch things around? Keep it the same? It doesn't matter. If he changes it, the next day will bring a whole new supply of ridicule. So, admirably, instead of picking up a pencil and paper and doodling Kilroy pictures, most managers strive to put the batting order together with a keen sense of thought. Every day the manager considers this task, weighing the strengths of his roster against the wit of the opposing team's pitcher and even the layout of that day's ballpark. Additionally, roster changes create flux of which managers have little control. This could include players moved on and off the disabled list (DL), trades to other teams or guys getting sent up from and down to the minor league teams.

Manager Bob Brenly went through a near constant search for the optimum combination for his 2003 Arizona Diamondbacks; his team Rolodexed through more than 140 different starting batting orders during the course of the 162-game season and still came up short when playoff berths were handed out. And this order instability is the norm. One of the most consistent teams was the 1984 Red Sox. Boston's manager used

forty-two batting orders en route to a number-four finish in the American League East that year.

A good benchmark for tweaking a lineup is whether a revised, hopefully better, lineup would produce ten extra runs a season, which sounds a bit underwhelming to us. But the theory goes something like this: ten extra runs would equate to one extra win a season. Got it. Now what? To a spectator, one extra win doesn't seem to be anything to get excited about. But many teams could use that one win to get into the playoffs or the World Series. For example, one game would have given the 1988 Tigers a shot at the playoffs. And an extra win for either Philadelphia or Cincinnati would have put their team in contention for the 1964 National League banner, which instead ended up going to the St. Louis Cardinals, the eventual world champions.

A lineup shake-up could have to do with moving people up and down the order or benching certain players to give others a chance. A left-handed opposing pitcher may lead a manager to change his lineup for the day, stacking it with a few choice right-handed batters, and reducing the number of left-handed hitters as much as possible. The manager may tap a backup player because he seems to perform better in a certain stadium or against a certain pitcher. Or on overcast Saturday nights in months that begin with "A." Then, there is perhaps the highest calling of all: a player's mom is in the stands. Get the Kleenex.

In the 1960s, before the DH was introduced, managers started to come up with inventive ways to tweak the lineup. It became popular to have a regular pinch hitter on the roster. The pinch hitter is sort of like the utility batter. Though this player may seem like a loser replacement, the job he fills is recognized as an unbelievably difficult one. Really, it's akin to being stuck having to replace the toner in the office copier. Could it have been you that one time who shirked that job? It's probably more like: who among us hasn't tried to walk away from that one?

Unlike the DH, the pinch hitter is not a regular in the lineup. Instead he is called in to hit at specific, often critical, moments in a game. All eyes are on him because he's supposed to be this great, Houdini of a clutch hitter—better than the guy he replaced, at least in this instance. But he doesn't even get the benefit of seeing the pitcher a few times to get a sense for his rhythm and speed. And pinch hitters get less practice time in the batting cage as compared to the starters. Sounds like this guy is set up to fail. But

this is what these guys do for a living. Batting on rare occasions, they exist out of the groove.

When the manager calls for a pinch hitter to come in to replace a batter, the guy who was originally in the lineup is benched for the rest of the game since, in baseball, once a player is pulled out he cannot return to the field. The pinch hitter effectively takes his position in the lineup and on the field. However, it is unlikely that a true pinch hitter will ever play in the field. After pinch hitters do—or fail at—what they are specifically called in to do, they are often replaced by a better defenseman who takes the field position and may continue hitting in that slot for the rest of the game.

Dusty Rhodes was a below-average player but had a knack in his role as a pinch hitter. The lefty was celebrated in 1954, when he earned the World Series MVP, hitting .667. This series included a walk-off home run by Rhodes in Game One, and the Giants swept the Cleveland Indians, outscoring them 21-9. In fact, Rhodes was such a force during the first three games of that series that *New York Herald Tribune* sportswriter Red Smith wrote that they were thinking of not even playing Game Four because Rhodes "may give an exhibition of walking on water."

But that kind of recognition is unusual, even for great career pinch hitters such as Lenny Harris, who had a lifetime average of .269 over eighteen seasons with eight different teams. Others with good pinch-hit records are Manny Mota, John Vander Wal, and Mark Sweeney. Much like utility fielders, these players work in relative obscurity.

When managers want to use a one-two punch on an opposing team, they may choose to open with the pinch hitter and then follow with a left hook: the pinch runner. Much like the pinch hitter, this player is brought in specifically because of his baserunning skill. Unlike Rickey Henderson, who was an all-around player who could run, hit, and field, pinch runners are not valued for their hitting or fielding. Rather, while other players may have several or all of the five tools that managers look for in a player (running, catching, throwing, hitting, and hitting for power), the pinch runner usually has only the running tool. In this way, the pinch runner makes up the other half of the whole offensive replacement that the manager called in: the pinch hitter hits and the pinch runner runs, yet neither one fields. Together they can be a formidable offensive unit. And, like the pinch hitter, you will rarely see a pinch runner staying in the game to field. He likely doesn't have the catching and throwing tools. That's if he even has a glove.

Oakland A's owner Charlie Finley signed twenty-two-year-old Herb Washington into the role of pinch runner for the 1974 and 1975 seasons. A world-class sprinter hailing from Michigan State University, Washington hadn't played baseball since high school, but Finley didn't care. The team needed a speedy baserunning specialist. Or so he imagined.

In 1974 Washington appeared in ninety-two games, scoring twenty-nine runs and stealing twenty-nine bases without wielding a bat once or having logged a single moment as a fielder. He was also pretty lucky, being in the right place at the right time when Oakland won the World Series that year, and he scored an embarrassingly huge ring. But Washington's instincts weren't sharp enough for the rigors of being a professional base stealer. Not only was he caught stealing sixteen times that year, his excitement occasionally got the better of him. Astute pitchers would pick him off when he took too big a lead in anticipation of stealing a base. One of that year's pick-off throws came from 1974 NL Cy Young winner Mike Marshall during that year's Dodgers-Oakland World Series. A reliever for the Dodgers, it also turns out that Marshall was Washington's physical education instructor at Michigan State. Just another case of college boys picking on college boys. What's next? Swirlies in the locker room?

Tony LaRussa is a modern manager who is known for his lineup shenanigans, sifting through his team roster in search of the slightest edge in any given ballgame scenario. Alvin Dark, the A's manager in the 1970s, would have different lineups depending on whether his team was behind or ahead in any given inning. Yankee manager Casey Stengel was known for his briefcase of hand-written lineup cards, and Baltimore's Earl Weaver would regularly wait until the last possible moment to turn in his lineup. This is the baseball world's version of corporate micro managing and situational planning.

To add more flex to the lineup, some managers practice lineup chicanery by loading their official batting orders with poor-hitting pitchers, of all things. On June 29, 1961, in the first game of a doubleheader between Philadelphia and San Francisco, both team's managers had righty and lefty pitchers warming up. Both were attempting to keep the opponent from figuring out which pitcher was going to start the game, preventing the other from finalizing his lineup.

This charade can go only so far, and Phillies manager Gene Mauch was finally required to turn in his lineup card to the umpire. But he had a plan,

although, on initial inspection, it didn't look much like a plan. His lineup strangely had four pitchers listed as batters and had them hitting first, third, seventh, and ninth. Now, from what we remember about lineups and pitchers, there are some glaring problems with this setup. A pitcher as the high on-base-percentage leadoff guy? Or as the high-average number-three hitter, often considered the best hitter on the team? If that isn't a cracked contrivance, we're not sure what is. And, according to Mauch's lineup card, the pitchers were the day's center fielder, right fielder, catcher, and the actual pitcher, who was predictably in the number-nine slot. Whew, at least he got one of them right.

As soon as Mauch saw that Alvin Dark, the Giants manager, was starting lefty Billy O'Dell, Mauch took all of the imposter pitchers out of his lineup and replaced them with genuine hitters—all right-handed batters— to battle the lefty O'Dell. After the Phillies' new leadoff replacement hit a single off O'Dell, Dark pulled his pitcher, replacing him with a righty to better challenge Mauch's new lineup. Oy. After about three hours of this behavior, the game ended when Willie Mays' solo home run in the top of the tenth broke the 7-7 tie.

There is really more to that day's story. Don Ferrarese, an average reliever with eight years in the majors, can tell his kids that he was once in the Philadelphia lineup as the leadoff hitter. He doesn't need to reveal the rest of the story. Let the kids look it up. That's a father's prerogative.

I followed baseball my whole life. But it wasn't until I started keeping score that I really started to learn about the game. Keeping score helped me to keep my attention on the game, formulate questions, track the season, and understand how the plays are made."

— *Carrie, 42*

SECTION SEVEN

Wanna Get Lucky?

$\mathcal{I}$f you've read this far, you've likely learned a lot. And we thank you for joining the ride! For those of you who skipped to this chapter, you missed some good stuff. But, hey, aren't we all looking for a few shortcuts in life? Either way, let's convert our quiet knowledge into something we can use. We bet you can now recognize some of the game's nuances. Or surely you're able to fill a painful lull during a business dinner with an entertaining story from this book. Or pick one of the boring stories. It's a business dinner, after all.

This last section of the book is about learning to score while you're watching a game. Many spectators approach scoring with trepidation or ignore it entirely. Well, let's confront the beast. One of the first things to learn is that there is no hopeless hurdle here. Don't get us wrong, we understand why scoring can look pretty intimidating. There are some fans who score games while secretively hovering over scorecards, their heads sandwiched between earphones. Looks like pretty serious stuff, huh? But we think that if Great Aunt Julia can score a game while tracking the gossip from the fans sitting behind her, ordering rounds of drinks, and maintaining her affable and amusing demeanor, then you can, too.

## CHAPTER 36

The Suggestions

The sooner you realize that the National Archives isn't going to call and demand that your scorecard be enshrined, the better. So, just relax. It can't be emphasized enough that there are far more suggestions than rules when it comes to scoring. There is no commission that exists solely to ensure every fan uses the same method and an agreed upon set of symbols. It's alright that some fans choose to score the stats for only one team while others . . . track . . . every . . . single . . . pitch thrown during a game.

For some, a perk to scoring a game is to be able to glance at the scorecard decades later and replay all the game-day action. For example, Deidre's dad still has his scorecard from the last game of the 1963 World Series in which the Los Angeles Dodgers' Sandy Koufax pitched against—and beat—the Yankees' Whitey Ford. It was a big year for Koufax, who also won that year's MVP, Cy Young, and the Triple Crown of pitching, a rare award achieved only when a pitcher leads the league or ties for the lead in strikeouts, wins, and ERA. While Dad's card has become a neat piece of memorabilia, you may have no desire to keep scorecards for more than forty years. That's okay; sometimes scoring just a game, a team, or only a couple

innings is its own goal. Why? Because it's different, enjoyable, and you will see some things on the field that you wouldn't ordinarily notice.

Additionally, you are not a failure if you missed something that happened on the field. What if you were busy cleaning cotton candy glop from your kid's face? No problem. Hall of Fame shortstop Phil Rizzuto came up with a symbol just for those times when life interferes with scoring. The symbol is "WW" and stands for "Wasn't Watching." Now, *that* could be fun to look back on in ten years! (Honey, look! This was when Little Suzy blew out her diaper, and, as I was changing her on the seat, I missed Hank Aaron's 715th home run. Damn kid.) Ah, memories. But, even if you missed a play, you might not need the "WW" symbol. This is because most MLB parks have a screen that lists how the last few plays panned out. If your stadium has something like that, you could play a little catch up that way. And you can always just turn around and ask the person behind you, "Hey, how did Polansky get on base?" Or, "Why is there a bone sticking out of his leg?" You may want to steer away from fans wearing headphones.

Fear of commitment needn't be an obstacle to scoring, either. It depends on how you choose to score. Every pitch? Sure, that's a commitment. It may also be fun. Looking for a little more down time? Try scoring only the home team. Perhaps you could make scoring a social event by alternating at bats with your kids. Or, decide ahead of time that you are going to score through only the fourth inning. Then toss the card in the recycle bin. Scorecards are a treasured possession to some, but they don't have to be to you. Maybe give yours to someone else to finish. You can also unceremoniously close your scorebook and pick up your kid or your drink—or both—and soak up the sunshine. Remember, you're at the ballgame. Be thankful you're not doing all the other things you're supposed to be doing.

If you do want to keep scorecards as records, you may want to buy a book that you can score games in all season long. You may even want to include additional information such as each player's batting average on that day. It could be interesting to look back on later in the season. And why not consider recording some of the things going on around you? The salacious gossip from two rows back. Put a note describing the deep meaning of the tangle of lines that your kid doodled over the eighth- and ninth-inning columns. You might want to write down the names of the friends you are with and those of the ones you just met. Maybe even remark about the day's weather. Are your feet hurting? Maybe it's the new shoes that you need to

remember not to wear again, but that might be hard to forget. The point here is that you're not one dimensional, and your scorecard doesn't need to be, either.

An old friend and big baseball fan was diagnosed with AIDS twelve years ago. He lived with my family for the last two-and-a-half years of his life; which coincided with my young son's early-baseball interest. In my friend's last minutes of life, we watched Pride of the Yankees with him. . . . It was October of 1995, and the Mariners were fantastic that season. I learned about baseball from my friend and became a "baseball mom" at the same time.

—Jeannie, 57

CHAPTER 37

Give Yourself a Fighting Chance

*A*s with any endeavor, you'll need the right equipment. Since the lesson today is about how to score, you'll need a scorecard. You can copy one off our website, use the *Savvy Girls' Scoring Journal*, or buy a different type of book to use when the urge strikes. Scorecards are also available at the games. You'll also need a pencil; one with an eraser works best, and a sharpener is handy to have, too, because a sharpened pencil will help keep your game information legible. Absent a sharpener, you can whittle your pencil into a point or opt to sharpen it on the concrete in front of you during the fourth inning. It's at about that time that the pencil will become dull, rendering your scorecard a smudged mess. You may also want to grab something to eat or drink. Once you get started scoring the game, you may not want to stop to get some of these game-day essentials.

Once you get settled into your seat, start writing down the day's lineup on your scorecard. Since managers may tweak their lineups until the last possible moment, you'll get the lineup information on your stadium's big screen.

You know, the Giant Screen. DinoVision. EnormoTele. Who knows what they call it in your neck of the woods. But it really doesn't matter. Nor does it matter how you get the information, just get it. Then transfer the info to your scorecard, writing each team on a different scorecard or on opposite sides of the same scorecard. As you write the players' names, leave a couple of lines under each so that you'll have space to write in a different name, should the starting player get replaced. Scorecards often provide extra room for this. Writing the lineup before the game begins will make keeping up with those early at bats easier, as they can come at you quickly. Writing the names is a task you can ask even a kid to do. If it's an older kid, perhaps she could do that while you run off for that beverage we seem to insist upon.

The scorecard has columns with numbers at the top of each that reflect the different innings, often going to the tenth. When someone comes up to bat, find the box that intersects with his name and the inning in which he is batting. Often, each box will have a diamond in it. It is here that you reflect what happened during that player's at bat, for better or worse. If he got on base, the same square can tell you what happened to him as the inning progressed. By the end of the game, you'll be able to see how many times a player got up to bat and how well he did. Depending on what else you choose to record, you can even tell where the batter tends to hit the ball (a lefty pulling the ball to right field is common). There is often space at the bottom of the scorecard for adding runs and other stats, as well as for including the stats for pitchers and catchers. It can get pretty involved, if you want it to.

You'll want to know the field positions in order to record how outs were made during the course of a game. As a reminder, each position on the defensive side has a number that corresponds to his position, one through nine. Here's a quick refresher course: the pitcher (1) and catcher (2) are the battery. The first baseman (3), second baseman (4), third baseman (5), and shortstop (6) are the infield. The left fielder (7), center fielder (8), and right fielder (9) are the outfield.

In addition to the fielding position numbers, other symbols will help you to keep track of things. After a player's at bat, you find the corresponding symbol to reflect what happened at his plate appearance. Here are examples of some commonly used symbols to reflect how a player got out:

K: The batter struck out. If the batter struck out while "looking" (i.e. he didn't swing at the third strike), then you'd put a backwards "Я."

6-3: This means the shortstop (6) fielded the hit ball and threw it to the first baseman (3) for the out. Adjust the numbers to whoever fielded the ball and whoever caught it for the out. If it was a double play, it might look like a 6-4-3. Sometimes outs are unassisted, such as when the first baseman gets the ground ball hit to him and steps on the base to get the runner out. This would be noted by using only "3," which would mean that he didn't need any help getting the out. Show off.

F8: The centerfielder catches a fly ball. The "F" means it was a fly out. The center field position is number eight. Here, you write down the number of the fielder who caught the ball. For example, if the right fielder caught the ball, it'd be a "F9." Sometimes it's a popup to the catcher. Then it'd be "F2." If you want to save space, you can just use the fielder's number, and the "F" is assumed. However, we like to use the "F" because it helps us distinguish a fly ball or pop up from an unassisted infield out—such as the one referring to the hotdog first baseman, above. If the first baseman caught a pop up for the out, we'd record that as an "F3." When it's a grounder, we'd write down only a "3." In this instance, the "F" helps identify the play. (Some scorers use the "F" to signify a caught foul ball, i.e., "F2," but we don't.) So, for aesthetics as much as consistency, we use the "F" in all fly-ball situations or pop ups, which are infield fly balls that sail high before being caught.

SF-9: This is a sacrifice fly that was caught by the right fielder (9). A different type of sacrifice play, the sac bunt, could be scored a little differently. For example, "SB 3-4" indicates that the bunt was picked up by the first baseman who then threw it to the second baseman to get the batter out at first. What's the second baseman doing at first base? He ran to "cover" first base while the first baseman rushed in to field the listless bunt. This type of fundamental backup defensive play makes it possible to get the out. Whether the out is a result of a fly ball or a bunt, it's called a sacrifice because the batter advanced the runner on base. You already know all that, right? Good job. But hold on a minute, scoring maven, you're not done, yet. The batter advanced the runner to second. Go back to the runner's "at bat" box that showed what happened during his at bat. We already know that he got on base. Now you can draw an extra line along the diamond to show which base he advanced to by virtue of the sacrifice bunt. If the runner makes it all the way around to score, you color in the diamond to show that his at bat resulted in a run.

When someone gets an out, not only will you indicate how he got out but it's also a good idea to specify which out it was in the inning. Do this by writing the out number inside a circle. This goes in the batter's square, along with the information reflecting how he got out. Be on the watch for when outs don't come with consecutive hitters. You'll see an example of when this would happen, which is often, when we do the scoring clinic in the next chapter.

But batters don't always get out! Here are some common examples to indicate how batters get on base, which, if you recall from earlier in the book, can be done by one of the seven following ways: a hit, a walk, hit by pitch, fielder's choice, catcher interference, error, or dropped third strike. Bravo, grasshopper!

As mentioned a couple paragraphs ago, when a batter gets on base, you can also track a runner's progress around the bases. You can reflect which base he stopped at each time by putting an extra mark—maybe a check-mark, an "x," anything!—everytime he stopped at a base. And if you color in his diamond when he gets around to score then it's easy to tell how many runs were scored in an inning. This is also a heads-up not to write anything inside the diamond if the batter gets on base. If he scores, you'll lose the information because you colored all over it.

Batter gets a hit; makes it to second base: You can record this by drawing a line around the diamond that corresponds with how far he went. You can write "2B" along either of the lines, to show he got a double. Or you can draw a couple hash marks across the basepath, one line for single, two for double, or three for triple.

Batter gets a walk: Otherwise known as a "Base on Balls," draw the line along the diamond to first base. Put a "BB" along the basepath so you'll know, forty years later, how he got on base. If he got there because the pitcher hit him with the pitch, you'd put in "HBP."

Batter gets on because of an error: This could be a situation when the batter hit a lazy ground ball to the shortstop who was dreaming about dental school as the ball rolled between his legs and into shallow right field. Or, he actually got to the ball and then threw it into the fifth row of fans sitting behind the first baseman who was waiting to catch the ball for the out. Either way, it's an error. Make a line along the diamond to the corner representing first base and write "E6" near it. That tells you it was an error on the focus-challenged shortstop.

Batter gets on base by a fielder's choice: This is when the fielders go for the easiest out and spare the other runner. You'll often see this when the defense is trying to turn a double play but fails. After getting the first out, which is usually a runner trying to get to second, the fielders sometimes can't get the batter out at first. Sometimes it's because the batter is really fast. Maybe the runner made a good slide into the second basemen's shins as the fielder tried to make the throw to first. Ouch! Whichever, had the fielders not gotten that first, easy out, they likely could have gotten the batter. But they made a choice. You'll see a couple of examples of this type of play in next chapter's scoring clinic. Draw a line to the first-base corner, and write "FC" for fielder's choice.

There are some generic markings that help collect other types of information. We use dots (•) at the bottom-left corner of the box to show if the batter got an RBI during that at bat. One little dot means he got one RBI, two dots means he hit two runners in to score, and so on. Additionally, you may want to mark the end of an inning with a hash (/) mark showing who was the last out. Some kind of mark makes it easier for you to see where the next inning starts. Since we like to know where a batter tends to hit, we track his hits by coloring in either corner to show that the ball went to left or right field. A dot in the middle of the upper part of the box signifies center field. If he got a hit to the shortstop, you can put a dot where the shortstop usually stands. We only do this with hits because our scoring already tells us where his outs went, by using the fielding number of the guy who caught the ball. We use an asterisk (*) to show when a pitching change happened. You may not decide to track too much pitching information, but writing down the starting pitcher would be considered a minimum. In the National League, he'll be in the batting order, anyway. There are spaces at the bottom of the scorecard in which to write the pitchers' names. When one is replaced, you could write down the new pitcher. If you want to track exactly when he came into the game, you can use the asterisk. Or, you can fill in the number of innings.

You could really go hog wild with this whole thing. Some fans track fouls, strikes, and balls with little dots in the batter's at-bat box. Devise a system that works for you. If the National Archives calls you up in the eighth inning, you would be able to tell them what the pitch count was when Polansky hit a homer in the second inning. You could, if you wanted, even tell Archives Wonk how many balls he fouled off in the fourth inning.

The possibilities are endless. Just a little warning: If you are too strict about recording the action on the field, you may be missing out on some action in the stands or with your companion. And there's no scorecard for the latter options. If you're with someone, try to remember why they are there.

When games go beyond ten innings, you have to get creative. But we trust you to do just that. Maybe being creative means grabbing another copy of the scorecard or making one up on your relish-stained hotdog napkin. Sometimes creativity means not being too picky. And just be happy you weren't scoring the May 9, 1984, twenty-five-inning game between the White Sox and Brewers that we mentioned in Chapter Nine: "Some of the Parts."

I have memories of being a teenager who went to school across from the Baltimore Orioles' stadium in 1957 and, because the windows were propped open, hearing the games during high school chemistry lab. I always wished I were across the street at the game instead of in the lab.

—Marion, 64

## CHAPTER 38

Let's Give It a Go

So, we thought we'd take an interesting game and break down a crucial inning for you. It is a game that was special to the two of us. We didn't go together but we were both glued to the action. Deidre was with her big brother in a New Mexico biker bar. She was there because the bar bore her last name. And she was thirsty. Jackie scored tickets to the game and went with her sister-in-law.

It was October, 1995, and our local team, the Seattle Mariners, was on a fine tear. Only two months earlier the team had been thirteen games out of playoff contention. The city had a rally cry, and the team responded, winning the American League West in a one-game playoff against a stunned California Angels team. The reward for winning that crucial game was facing the AL wild card-winning Yankees in a five-game series. Winning that series would give the Mariners a shot at the AL pennant. Now, it is important to know that the 1995 Yankees were not yet the team that we've all come to love and loathe. It was in the following year that Joe Torre joined as manager and Derek Jeter won the Rookie of the Year leading the Yankees to the team's first championship in eighteen years. Three more World Series victories for the Yankees followed in the next four years. But that doesn't

mean the Yanks weren't good in 1995—they were. And the Mariners were underwhelming underdogs.

The Yankees won the first two games in the Bronx and then headed to Seattle's cavernous Kingdome to win one more and close the deal. But it didn't work out that way. The Mariners took the first game, and the second one. Going into Game Five, the Yankees were up against the wall. Of course, so were the Mariners. It was quite a set up.

The visiting Yankees were first up to bat, leading off with Wade Boggs. He struck out (K). Barry Williams met with a similar fate (K). Paul O'Neill came up to bat with a .300 batting average and flew out to the left fielder (F7). Three batters up, and three down. Next came the Mariners, whose first three batters fared no better. So, the first inning was a bust. When the Yankees came up at the top of the second, it was again three up and three down. We're starting to wonder whether the fan scoring with his headphones on isn't instead listening to National Public Radio. When the Mariners batted in the bottom of the inning, they showed some spunk but closed out the inning with no runs scored and two runners left on base (LOB). Then came the Yankees . . . Wait! We're starting to sound like those annoying commentators who talk incessantly, never giving you a chance to see something for yourself. But we know you're pretty savvy. Check out the scorecards on the next two pages and relive the action that mesmerized fans from the Atlantic to the Pacific that fine autumn day in 1995. Game on!

So, after the tenth inning, your scorecard may look something like the cards on those two pages. Well, that's if you are a messy scorer like Deidre. But there are no mustard stains—so consider yourself lucky. What can you tell from these obscure markings? Well, first that it's a game in an American League stadium, because there is a DH listed in the lineup. Actually, since the teams were vying for a chance to play for the AL pennant, both teams were in the AL and have a DH. Ruben Sierra was the chosen one for the Yankees, and Edgar Martinez hit for the Mariners.

A glance at the scorecard will also reveal a flurry of replacements. The seventh slot for the Mariners was filled by five different players. Warren Newson was brought in to pinch hit for the Mariners' starting shortstop Luis Soho in the bottom of the sixth. There were two out and Edgar Martinez was on second base. The plan was for Newson to get a hit so Edgar could score. But Newson never got on base; rather, he struck out. And he never got to play the field, either. Instead, he was replaced by a

Visitor: NY	Home: Sea	Weather: Dome	Notes: but it's nice outside!	Date: 10-8-95	Game Time: yes

TEAM: YANKEES

#	Line Up	Pos	1	2	3	4	5	6	7	8	9	10	AB	R	H	RBI
	Boggs	3B	①K			F7		X	② 3-1		①K					
	B. Williams	CF	②K								②F4					
	O'Neill	RF	③F7			HC			③F7	③F2						
	Sierra	DH		①F8		②F8				①K	①K					
	Mattingly	1B		②F7		③F9		X		②F7	②X					
PR/6	James Williams	LF / LF		③3		③3①	W		③ 6-4	③X						
	Stanley	C			①X 6-3		②5-3	②F-2		RC						
	Fernandez	SS			②6-3		X	③F7			X					
	Velarde	2B			②X	③F2		①X								

S	Runs	0	0	0	2	0	2	0	0	0	0				
U	Hits	0	0	1	1	1	1	0	2	0					
M	Errors	0	0	0	0	0	0	0	0	0	0				
S	LOB	0	0	0	0	1	3	1	1	2	0				

#	Pitchers	IP	H	R	BB	SO	HB
	CONE						
*	RIVERA						
**	McDOWELL						

IP: innings pitched
H: hits
R: runs
BB: Base on Balls
SO: Strikeouts
HB: Hit Batters

LOB: The number of runners left on base at the end of the inning. These are potential runs that never scored.

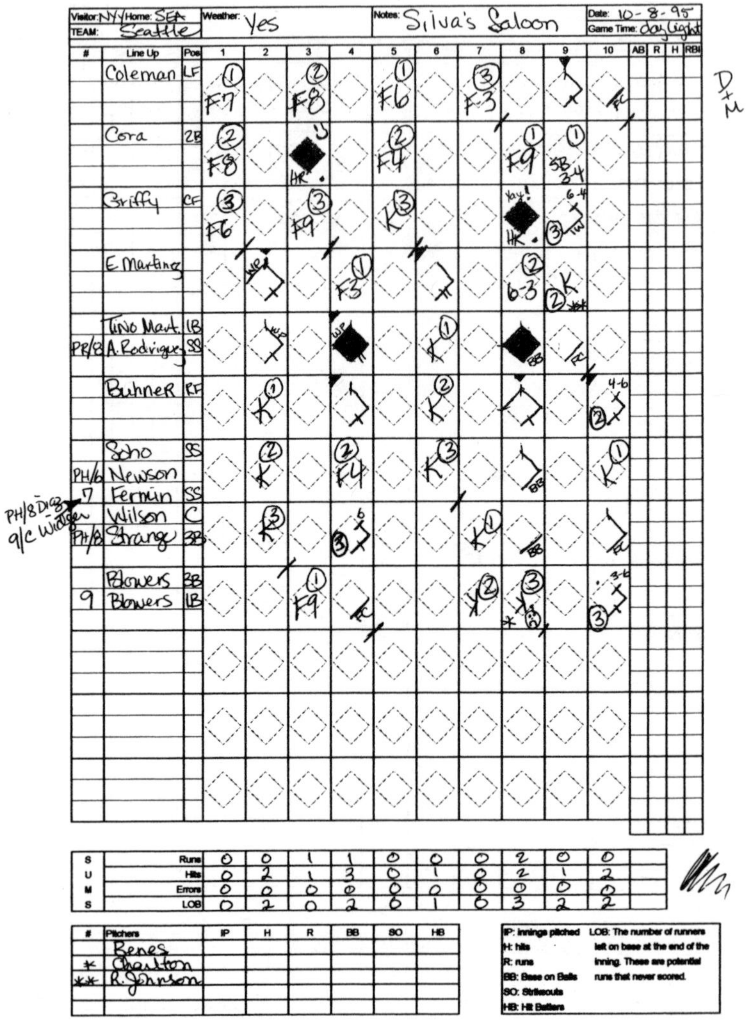

This page is a baseball scorecard.

| Visitor: N.Y. / Home: SEA | TEAM: Seattle | Weather: Yes | | | | Notes: Silva's Saloon | | | Date: 10-8-95 | Game Time: day light | | | | | |

D + M

#	Line Up	Pos	1	2	3	4	5	6	7	8	9	10	AB	R	H	RBI
	Coleman	LF	① F7	② F8		① F6		③ F3							
	Cora	2B	② F8		HR	② F4			① F9	① SB 3-4					
	Griffy	CF	③ F6		③ K9	K③			HR	③	6-4				
	E. Martinez					F3 ①			② 6-3	② K					
	Tino Mart. / PR/8 A. Rodriguez	1B / SS					①			SS					
	Buhner	RF		① K			② K				4-6 ②				
	Soto / PH/6 Newson / Fermin	SS / SS	② K	② F4		K③			SS	① K					
7	Wilson / PH/8 Strange	C / 3B	③ K		③		①	SS							
9	Blowers / Blowers	3B / 1B		① F9	K		②	③ K	③	3-6 ③					

PH/8 D3 / 9/c Widger / PH/8

		Runs	○	○	|	|	○	○	○	2	○	○		
S	Runs		○	○	1	1	○	○	○	2	○	○		
U	Hits		○	2	1	3	○	1	○	2	1	2		
M	Errors		○	○	○	○	○	○	○	○	○	○		
S	LOB		○	2	○	2	○	○	○	3	2	2		

#	Pitchers	IP	H	R	BB	SO	HB
	Benes						
*	Charlton						
**	R. Johnson						

IP: innings pitched
H: hits
R: runs
BB: Base on Balls
SO: Strikeouts
HB: Hit Batters

LOB: The number of runners left on base at the end of the inning. These are potential runs that never scored.

better fielder, Felix Fermin, to play shortstop while the Yankees were at bat in the top of the seventh. But when it came time for Fermin to bat, he was replaced in the bottom of the eighth inning by pinch hitter Alex Diaz, who was walked to first base, and then again to second, before the inning ended. After all of that excitement, Diaz never played the field! Instead, Mariner manager Lou Piniella put in Chris Widger to play catcher in the top of the ninth inning. The Widger replacement snowballed into a slew of other position changes. Alex Rodriguez, who was called in to pinch run for first baseman Tino Martinez in the eighth inning, played shortstop. But then the team was missing a guy to play first. This was fixed by bringing in Doug Strange to play third base and moving Mike Blowers from third base to first. Whew. Since there wasn't enough room on the scorecard, a couple names went in the margin. We're starting to think that team managers fail to consider the scoring public when they make such decisions. So messy!

During and after the game, review your scorecard and see how many players were left on base. These are the runners whose teammates were unable to hit them in to score. Oh, woe! Indeed, if your favorite team lost a close game, you really need to be in the right frame of mind to view this information. By the end of the Yankees-Mariners game, New York left ten players on base and Seattle stranded thirteen. Think of how different the game would have been if only a couple of those runners scored! Where is the clutch hitting, you ask? Remember, clutch players are the ones tasked with racking up a few RBI in tense and decisive moments. Well, that's if such a hitter exists. But, if he does exist, you'll sense his presence in the bottom of the eleventh inning.

Things were looking good for the Yankees until the Mariners tied the game, 4-4, with two runs in the bottom of the eighth inning. But New York had faced some tricky situations before that point in the game. In the second inning, for example, the Mariners had one out and runners on second and third, care of a wild pitch (WP) from Yankee pitcher David Cone, which advanced both Edgar and Tino. Then Cone delivered two more strikeouts, ending the inning. Then, in the bottom of the eighth inning, Cone put himself in a vice by walking Doug Strange with the bases loaded. This gaffe allowed pinch runner Alex Rodriguez to score the tying run. Cone's collapse led to his removal from the game. Mariano Rivera replaced him, striking out Mike Blowers, the ninth batter and a .257 hitter that year, for the final out of the inning.

Cone wasn't the only one suffering; the Mariners had their own pitching hardships to deal with. A particular string of missteps helped the Yankees score two runs in the top of the sixth inning. After starter Andy Benes got Wade Boggs called out on strikes (𝗞), he walked the bases loaded and gave up a two RBI double to Don "Donnie Baseball" Mattingly. To show this achievement, we gave Mr. Baseball two RBI dots in his at bat square. But, as Mariners fans, we didn't want to.

There are lots of things you can tell from a scorecard. After striking out in the first inning, the Yankees' number-two hitter, Bernie Williams, was walked four times during the eleven-inning game. And he scored twice—in the fourth and sixth innings. And after the Mariners' starter seemed to have the seventh inning in hand, Benes got sloppy and walked Williams. Perhaps hoping to avoid a breakdown like the one that led to Mattingly's double in the sixth inning, Benes was quickly replaced by Norm Charlton. In the ninth inning Charlton let two guys on base with none out. This situation—ninth inning, game tied, a guy in scoring position, another on base, and no outs—was too close for comfort for the Mariners skipper, Piniella. The manager called for his ace pitcher, Randy Johnson, who took over for Charlton in a rare relief appearance. A team's dominant starter will occasionally relief pitch during important games, such as this one.

You can even see a few spots where the defense set up the double play. In the ninth inning, Vince Coleman led off the bottom of the inning with a single to center field. Joey Cora advanced Coleman with a sacrifice bunt that was fielded by the first baseman, who threw it to the second baseman (SB 3-4) covering first for the out. With less than two outs, no one on first, and a man on second, Griffey was walked to set up the double play. Here you have offensive small ball (the sacrifice) and the defensive counter punch (the intentional walk). But then Edgar Martinez, the Mariners' number-four hitter, struck out. Now, with two out, the defense was no longer looking for a double-play ball; they needed only one out to end the inning. Enter Alex Rodriguez, who pinch ran for Tino Martinez in the bottom of the eighth and came to bat with two out and two on base. With the game tied, he could have won it right there by scoring the speedy Coleman, who was on second, with a base hit. Quite a heady situation for the youngster; perhaps too heady. Rodriguez hit to the shortstop who threw to the second baseman (6-4) to get Griffey for the force and the last out of the inning. We showed this final out by drawing a hacked-off line up the "basepath" to

second base and giving Griffey a big, fat "**3**" in his box. This is a place where you see that the outs didn't always come in consecutive at bats. The number-three hitter (Griffey) got out after the number-four hitter (Martinez). Even though the inning was over, Alex's at bat was scored a fielder's choice (FC), and he's counted as one of the two runners left on base at the end of the inning. Vince Coleman, the leadoff, was the other runner stranded.

Mike Blowers was the Mariners number-nine hitter and the one who started off the third inning. The next hitter, Coleman, was the team's lead-off and at the top of the list. Since Coleman was still batting in the third inning it was important to keep his stats in that column. So, as you see it on this scorecard, his at bat in the third inning goes straight above Blowers' at bat. Then Cora's and Griffey's stats go below Coleman's. If Blowers came up to bat again in the third, it would be called "batting around the order." In that hypothetical case, you would have to put Blowers' second at bat of the inning in the next column, scratching out the "4" at the top of the column and replacing it with a "3." Then you'd have to adjust the numbers of all the other columns. Since batting around the order doesn't happen too frequently and since most scorecards give space for an extra inning, your card can stay relatively neat. That is, unless the game goes into extra innings, in which case, you'd run out of space on your original card. Otherwise, you can always keep things tidy by using extra scorecards. In many respects, this game was pretty clean.

So, let's work our way through the climactic eleventh inning. Since all the space was used up on our first scorecard, we started a new one. You may or may not have the benefit of an additional card. We, on the other hand, have had more than a decade to prepare for this scoring clinic moment, so Jackie managed to scrounge up the necessary extra materials. If you don't have an extra card, get creative. After all, this may be one of those games you want to turn back to when Little Suzy is in college.

After Randy Johnson shut down the Yankees in the top of the tenth, they came back mad. Mike Stanley, the Yankees' catcher, got a walk to first. Okay, so maybe they weren't crazy mad. After Stanley got on base, he was replaced by pinch runner Pat Kelly. Tony Fernandez's sacrifice bunt put Kelly into scoring position. And score he did. Kelly put the Yankees in the lead by scoring off Randy Velarde's single to left field, and Velarde displayed some heads up baserunning, too! The Mariners were consumed with stopping Kelly's go-ahead run and threw the ball home in an effort to get him

Visitor: NYY Home: Sea	Weather:	Notes:	Date: 10-8-95
TEAM: Yankees	Most certainly ... but I can't see it!		Game Time:

#	Line Up	Pos	1	2	3	4	5	6	7	8	9	10	AB	R	H	RBI
	Boggs	3B	②													
PH/11	Leyritz	C														
	B. Williams	CF														
	O'Neill	RF	③													
	Sierra	DH														
	Mattingly	1B														
	James	LF														
PR/6	Williams	LF														
	Stanley	C	yikes!													
PR/11	Kelly	2B	3B													
	Fernandez	SS	① SB 3 4													
	Velarde	2B 3B														

S U M S	Runs	1
	Hits	1
	Errors	0
	LOB	2

#	Pitchers	IP	H	R	BB	SO	HB
	Cone						
	Rivera						
	McDowell						

IP: Innings pitched
H: hits
R: runs
BB: Base on Balls
SO: Strikeouts
HB: Hit Batters

LOB: The number of runners left on base at the end of the inning. These are potential runs that never scored.

| Visitor: NYY Home: Sea | Weather: Sunny + Warm | Notes: I'm really in N.M. | Date: 10-8-95 |
| TEAM: Seattle | | | Game Time: |

#	Line Up	Pos	1	2	3	4	5	6	7	8	9	10	AB	R	H	RBI
	Coleman	LF														
	Cora	2B	BUNT													
	Griffey	CF														
	E. Martinez	DH	THE DOUBLE!													
	TNO	1B														
	Buhner	RF	Game Over!													
	Sho	SS														
PH/6	Newson															
7	Fermin	SS														
PH/8 D#33	Wilson	C														
9/C L#08 PH/8	Strange	3B														
	Blowers	3B														
11		1B														

			1	2	3	4	5	6	7	8	9	10
S		Runs	2									
U		Hits	3									
M		Errors	0									
S		LOB	1									

#	Pitchers	IP	H	R	BB	SO	HB
	Bones						
*	Charlton						
**	Randy						

IP: innings pitched
H: hits
R: runs
BB: Base on Balls
SO: Strikeouts
HB: Hit Batters

LOB: The number of runners left on base at the end of the inning. These are potential runs that never scored.

out—a good play for the Mariners. However, Velarde took second base—a good play for the Yankees. And, now, he was in scoring position. But that's where the inning ended. For the Yankees, it was a success!

It was a short-lived victory. The Mariners put together an efficient and flawless bottom half. Joey Cora got on base with a bunt! In the third inning he hit a solo home run. And now we find out that he knows how to scrape out a base hit bunt, too? Then, Griffey hit a single to center and Cora took third base. From there, Cora could easily score on a base hit and tie the game, and there were no outs. Things were looking good as Edgar Martinez came up to bat. (Things often looked good when Edgar came up to bat.) He hit a long ball to left field for a double. Cora scores! The game was tied. Hooray! We'd see more baseball that night. Well, maybe not. Look! Griffey was still on the move. He rounded third and didn't look like he was going to stop. And he was the go-ahead run, the game winner. Will he make it?!? Well, having looked at the scorecard, you already know. And it happened more than ten years ago, so there is really no drama to add.

Wow. What a game! Hope you found it as thrilling as we did. Deidre and her brother had to call their Dad, the hoarder from the Sandy Koufax 1963 scorecard fame, to drive them home from the biker bar that was teeming with Yankees' fans. Oh, get your cynical minds out of the gutter! It was not because they'd had too much to drink; they just didn't have a car. Jackie had a car but lived within walking distance of the Kingdome, so wheels were irrelevant. As for the Mariners? The team went on to lose to the Cleveland Indians in the American League Championship Series (ALCS), a team run by manager Mike Hargrove. Hargrove took over the helm in Seattle ten years later. Coincidence? Yes.

Why do I like baseball? The whole game is just a series of great skills and artistry in motion.

—Connie, 32

Épilogue

Always Remember Where You Came From

*N*ot to get too philosophical on you but, really, who among us hasn't wondered how we got here? Well, aside from the stories that involve poison apples or birds and bees, it's a bit unconventional. While baseball's various daddies wrestled over the carpool schedule, Jack Norworth busied himself with other pressing matters. We like to imagine that he took a couple of his passions and put them to music. But there's no point in adding any more baseball fables to your list, so we won't get too fanciful. What we do know is that Norworth was inspired by a billboard advertising a ball game at the Polo Grounds in 1908. While that may inspire some of us to continue on our way, make some dinner, and go to bed, Norworth composed a song. He wrote it on a scrap of paper while riding the New York City subway. It was about a woman who, when her boyfriend offered to take her to a show, said, "No, I'll tell you what you can do . . ."

"Take Me Out to the Ball Game"

Yes, the song embraced by fans in baseball stadiums across the country is really only the refrain to a song written about a woman, Katie Casey, who was, "baseball mad, who had the fever, and had it bad." The words were changed somewhat in 1927, but it remained a song about a woman itching to take in a game. Norworth himself didn't attend his first game until many years later.

Other songs about baseball came and went, but it was this one about a woman wanting to go to the game that made a lasting mark on the national pastime. It was arguably Harry Caray's throaty rendition during the Cubs' seventh-inning stretch that brought the song into the public's consciousness after it had been pretty much forgotten for fifty years.

So, thanks Jack. Thanks Harry. And thanks Katie. That's for helping to give female fans a comfortable place in the world of baseball. Many, like us, have found that going to games can be a nice way to spend the day. We've learned that baseball can be fun to read about. And tracking whatever

baseball information that may interest you can be a rewarding pastime in itself. Lord knows, the game's unending stream of numbers and names offers plenty to satisfy the most unrepentant detective in any of us.

And one of the things we most enjoy is that our time in the stands folds out as easily—and sometimes as dramatically—as the action on the field, and we've got the stories to show for it. Like a lot of fans, our baseball stories have little to do with the players. Some of these stories are borne from allowing our brains to flatline during the game. Then what comes out of our mouths is pretty amusing. But that's not to say we can't be pretty engaging, too! We'll share a score card, a little chatter, and some drinks. And, yes, we've had our ugly fan moments. Take your pick. One of our favorites is the proverbial cellphone call to the friends in a nearby section. Cue ridiculous and obnoxiously loud conversation. "We're in front of the guy with the pink sweater! No—not the bald guy," we yell and wave wildly for them to see us. "Two rows down. See us? Hiiiiiiii!" So, maybe we aren't "true" fans. Certainly, after confessing to having made the irritating call, many would politely decline to comment. Others wouldn't be as polite. Definitely not true fans, they'd decree. But don't we get bonus points for spending three years writing a baseball book? Come on. Surely, that must help our standing for those tracking the fan-o-meter. Ok, maybe we are simply "real" fans? Hmmm. Is that a demotion from a "true" fan? Probably like you, we're hard to pigeon-hole. So, don't let anyone get uppity about questioning your fan status. And if they do, state your mind, then run like hell. Remember: if only in spirit, which is best in such dicey sitations, we're behind you all the way.

Hey, what are friends for?

$\mathcal{S}$ources

Anderson, Dave. "Sports of the Times: Manager Issues a Foolish Challenge." *The New York Times.* 12 June 1999. *ProQuest Historical Newspapers* (online). (24 Jan. 2007).

Andriesen, David. "During a game, first base is social hub for major leaguers." *Baseball Digest.* Sept. 2002. *findarticles.com* (online). (18 Dec. 2006).

Attner, Paul. "Four men, four sports, one link." *The Sporting News.* 12 Dec. 1994. *Encylopedia.com* (online). (14 Jan. 2007).

Bouton, Jim. Telephone Interview. 28 March 2007.

Conner, Floyd. *Baseball's Most Wanted* (New Jersey: Galahad Books, 2006).

Conner, Floyd. *Baseball's Most Wanted II* (Washington, D.C.:Brassey's, Inc. 2003).

Dickson, Paul. *The New Dickson Baseball Dictionary* (San Diego: Harcourt Brace & Company, 1999).

Doyle, Al. "Former Boston Red Sox infielder Marty Barrett: second baseman recalls 1986 season when he captured MVP honors in the American League Championship Series against the California Angels." *Baseball Digest.* August 2002. *findarticles.com* (online) (14 Jan. 2007).

Gillette, Gary and Peter Palmer. *The 2006 ESPN Baseball Encyclopedia* (New York: Sterling Publishing, 2006).

Goldman, Steven. "You Could Look It Up." *Baseball Prospectus* (7 Jul. 2004. 2 Apr. 2007).

Gorman, Lou. Telephone Interview (2 Jan. 2007).

Gorman, Lou. Telephone Interview (12 Feb. 2007).

Hemond, Roland. Telephone Interview (12 Feb. 2007).

"The History of Chavez Ravine." Independent Lens. *pbs.org* (10 March 2007).

Holtzman, Jerome. "Baseball Integration." *Encyclopedia Britannica* (14 Dec. 2006).

Horton, Willie. *The People's Champion* (Michigan: Immortal Investments Publishing, 2005).

James, Bill. *The New Bill James Historical Baseball Abstract* (New York: Free Press, 2001).

Jenkinson, Bill. *The Year Babe Ruth Hit 104 Home Runs* (New York: Carroll & Graf Publishers, 2007).

Kindred, Dave. "A face to remember." *The Sporting News.* 14 June 1999. *Encyclopedia.com* (online) (18 March 2007).

Hagen, Paul and John Kruk. *"I Ain't an Athlete, Lady . . ."* (New York: Simon & Schuster 1994).

Light, Jonathan Fraser. *The Cultural Encyclopedia of Baseball* (North Carolina: McFarland & Company 2005).

Lowry, Philip J. *Green Cathedrals.* (New York: Walker & Company, 2006.)

"MLB Baseball 2006 Salaries." *sportsline.com.* (8 Feb. 2007.)

Mackin, Bob. *The Unofficial Guide to Baseball's Most Unusual Records* (Vancouver, British Columbia: Douglas & McIntyre Publishing Group, 2004).

Maraniss, David. *Clemente: The Passion and Grace of Baseball's Last Hero* (New York: Simon & Schuster 2006).

Marazzi, Rich. "Baseball Rules Corner." *Baseball Digest.* Oct. 2001. *findarticles.com* (online) (2 Oct. 2006).

Morris, Peter. *A Game of Inches: The Game on the Field* (Chicago: Ivan R. Dee, 2006).

Morris, Peter. *A Game of Inches: The Game Behind the Scenes* (Chicago: Ivan R. Dee, 2006).

Okrent, Daniel and Steve Wulf. *Baseball Anecdotes* (New York: HarperPerennial, 1990).

Oliver, Nate. Personal interview (17 March 2006).

Port, Mike. Telephone interview (12 Feb. 2007).

Purdy, Dennis. *The Team by Team Encyclopedia of Major League Baseball* (New York: Workman Publishing, 2006).

"Quake Shakes San Francisco." *cbsnews.com.* 14 May 2002. 11 Nov. 2006.

Quigley, Martin. *The Crooked Pitch* (Chapel Hill: Algonquin Books, 1988).

Ritter, Lawrence S. *The Glory of Their Times* (New York: The MacMillan Company, 1966).

Ryan, Joan. "Flood's Fight Wasn't About The Money." *San Francisco Chronicle.* 22 Jan. 1997. 14 Dec. 2006

Schlossberg, Dan. "When Carl Yastrzemski became a star." *Baseball Digest.* July, 2002. *findarticles.com* (online) (2 April 2007).

"Schmelz at the Helm." *The Washington Post.* 3 Aug. 1896: 8. *ProQuest Historical Newspapers* (online). (17 Jan. 2007).

Seror, Marc. "If They Get Hit, It's Their Fault." *thegloryofbaseball.blogspot. com.* 1 March 2005.

Sheldon, Mark. "Aurilia keys Reds' comeback win." *Offical Site of the Cincinnatti Red*s. 22 August 2006. 22 March 2007.

Soloman, Burt. *The Baseball Timeline* (New York: DK Publishing, 2001).

Thorn, John. "Four Fathers of Baseball" *Thornpricks.blogspot.com* (16 July 2005).

http://www.thornpricks.blogspot.com/2005/07/four-fathers-of-baseball. html (23 March 2007).

Thorn, John. "The Charm of the Game." mrbaseball.com.

Thorn, John, et al. *Total Baseball: The Official Encyclopedia of Major League Baseball (7th ed).* New York: Warner Books, 2004.

Vass, George. "Juggling The Lineup." *Baseball Digest.* Jan. 2001. *findarticles. com* (online). (8 Feb 2007).

Veltrop, Kyle. *The Sporting News.* 21 June 2004. *findarticles.com* (online) (7 Feb. 2007).

Verducci, Tom. "Change is good." *Sports Illustrated.* 15 July 2003. 24 Jan. 2007.

"Waiting for Dusty." *time.com.* 11 Oct. 1954. 2 Feb. 2007.

Wilbur, Eric. "Passed isn't present." *Boston.com.* 1 May 2006.

 224  It Takes More Than Balls

Williams, Pete. "Frequent Fliers." *Street & Smith's Sports Business Journal.* 13 March 2006. 28 March 2007.
http://www.petewilliams.net/SBJFlying.htm
Young, Bob. "Gaylord Perry enjoys the Kenny Rogers rhubarb." *The Arizona Republic.* 24 Oct. 2006. *usatoday.com* (online). (12 Jan. 2007).

Frequently used Websites:
Baseball Almanac: www.baseball-almanac.com
The Baseball Biography Project (Society for American Baseball Research): www.bioproj.sabr.org
The Baseball Page: www.thebaseballpage.com
Baseball Library: www.baseballlibrary.com
Baseball Reference: www.baseball-reference.com
Baseball Think Factory: www.baseballthinkfactory.com
ESPN: www.espn.com
The Fielding Bible: www.fieldingbible.com
The National Baseball Hall of Fame and Museum: www.baseballhalloffame.org
The Official Site of Major League Baseball: www.mlb.com
Retrosheet: www.retrosheet.org
Society For American Baseball Research (SABR): www.sabr.org
Time magazine: www.time.com/time

Frequently used publications:
The Sporting News
Sports Illustrated
The New York Times
The Washington Post

$\mathcal{A}cknowledgments$

$\mathcal{S}$pecial thanks to Michael, John, Judy, Marc, Jennifer, Amelia, and Tony.

We have so many others to thank—too many to include here. So we decided to write everyone's name down on a piece of paper and put them in Deidre's cool cowboy hat. We pulled out names until we had calluses and papercuts. If you didn't make the list this time, we're sorry. But our excuse is that we're rookies. Not like a Fred Lynn rookie—we're real rookies. Look for your name in the next book when we've fine tuned things a bit.

Rebecca Hale, Polansky, Dave Baldwin, Barbara Rosenberg, Jonathan Schmidt, Lou Gorman, Michelle Peterman, Rich the parking lot guy in Vero Beach, Florida, Trisha Mills, Ron Kaplan, Gerry Silva, Mark Weinstein, Sally Hulsman, Mike Henderson, R.J. Lesch, Nate Oliver, Dave Birmingham, Aunt Donna, Overton Berry, Callie and Brooksie, Ben Barton, Jaime Weber, Trina Robinson, J.J. Redwolf, Keith Wetzler, Pam DeKeyser, Great Aunt Julia, Ryan Taylor, Roland Hemond, Little Suzy, Kieren Dutcher, Mike Rice, Nicole Brodeur, Lauren Griswold, Jeff Angus, Laurie Mathews, Ray Oducayen, Lisa Keller, Stephen Kern, Ken Mitchell, Leslie David, Ellen Eskanazi, Jennifer Campanile, Chris Moore, Bonnie

Faircloth, Aunt Beans, Shannon Follett, Mike Port, Emily Christy, Alan Schwarz, Mr. Horton, Steve Steinberg, Tony and Deb Pilotto, Charlie West, Jill Koney Daly, Gregg Greene, Lee Rosco, Art Thiel, Cindy and Steve Saunders, Schelleen Rathkopf, Nana, Nancy Haver, Eve Soffler, Andrew McCullough, Athima Chansanchai, Kris Hussey, Rick Griswold, Marya McCabe, Nathan and Jill in Peoria, Tom D'Angelo, Rita Dybdahl Cline, Marcia Littlejohn, Jen Hurtarte, Aunties Gina and Kathy, Greg the parking lot guy in Peoria, Tom Koney, NY Gary, Jim Moore, Roger DeWitt, Pearl, Lisa Denis-Gustaveson, Eric Riddle, Bonnie Bizzell, Bill Abelson, Judy Hill, Kris Kucera, Bob and Sheri, and Jimbo.

Index